Maybe Tomorrow

A Hidden Child of the Holocaust

Maybe Tomorrow

A Hidden Child of the Holocaust

Eric Cahn

by Eric Cahn

as told to Marilyn Saltzman

Acknowledgements

The authors express their appreciation for the love and support
of Jane, Kevin, Michelle and Jeff Cahn; Irv, Heidi and Kevin
Saltzman; Molly Bresler; Neva Cahn; Pauline Duffy;
Jack Gershtenson; Judy Gilbert Lazar; Bob Perkins;
Ray Resnick; Chuck Toft; and Sol and Rene Schwartz.

Special thanks to Vickie Bane, Teresa Ford, and Allison
St. Claire for their counsel on this project.

Author's Note

This book is based on the life experiences of Eric Cahn. In some
cases, names have been changed on request.

Cover design by Stortz Design,
Evergreen, Colorado
Book Design by Dianne Borneman, Shadow Canyon Graphics,
Evergreen, Colorado

Printed in the United States of America

Casan Publishing Company
P.O. Box 642
Arvada, Colorado 80001-0642

Contents

DEDICATED TO JOHANNA PLAUT CAHN
MARCH 31, 1913 – SEPTEMBER 18, 1942

With Deepest Gratitude

To the unidentified French Christian family who risked their lives to provide refuge to a four-year-old Jewish boy, Heinz Erich Cahn, in 1942.

To the Oeuvre de Secours aux Enfants in France, who rescued Erich from the Nazis and found him a safe haven.

Chapter One

My Mother's Corner

The sun peeks through the vertical blinds of my office, warming the shoulders of my gray flannel suit as I face the stark landscape hanging in my mother's corner. The water-color, leafless trees in a field of fresh snow, sends shivers down my spine. Nearby, bare twigs the color of burnt sienna rise three feet above a tall ceramic vase, echoing the painting's desolation.

This afternoon, teetering under the weight of life's burdens, I am drawn to this corner. Its peach-colored walls surround me like a mother's arms embracing a crying child. I silently seek solace for the little boy inside who lost his mother at the age of four.

The turbulent years I spent with my mother, Johanna "Hannah" Plaut Cahn, are little more than a blur in my memory. I don't recall my mother's touch, and I cannot picture her face as she held me. Yet in this corner, my mother's strength engulfs me. I celebrate her hope for a better tomorrow, and I mourn her death.

This corner of my office, with its barren landscape and the denuded twigs, mirrors the chill of my mother, Hannah's, arrival at Auschwitz on September 18, 1942. How terrified she must have been as she and my father were pushed from the box cars and sent in opposite directions. Together they had borne years of horror under the Nazi regime, and now came the final pain of separation. Hannah wondered if she would ever see Julius again as she was sent off to the left side of the tracks. The frost of fear in Hannah's heart did not last long; she didn't survive the hour. The Gestapo herded her straight from the railroad siding to the gas chamber.

Hannah's short life was marked by violence and loss. She was born to an unwed mother on March 31, 1913. Twenty-nine years later, after being ripped from all she loved, she was murdered by Hitler's henchmen.

Hannah spent her early years surrounded by aunts and uncles. Her mother, Rachel Plaut (Oma), brought the baby home to her father's house. Great Grandfather Plaut, twice a widower, needed Oma's help with his half-orphaned brood. One by one, the aunts and uncles grew up and left Oma, Hannah — and Germany — behind. The Plaut children had heard about the promise of America, and they set off to find a new life in the new world.

In 1920, when Hannah was seven, Oma met and married a World War I hero, Herman Adler, known to me as Opa. They settled in the rural area of Obervorschutz to raise their rapidly growing family of six children plus Hannah. The Adlers were the only Jews in town, and they struggled to survive as Opa's business ventures became rituals of failure.

Opa never adopted Hannah, and she kept the surname Plaut. As soon as Hannah turned fourteen, she was considered old enough to work. She was dispatched to Hamburg to serve as a cook for a well-known rabbi.

With the devotion of the first-born, Hannah regularly mailed money home to Oma and Opa. Her sense of responsibility for the family marked all she did, and her letters were full of love and concern for the half-brothers and sisters still left at home.

Hannah also wanted to protect herself. She saw in the big city of Hamburg that Hitler was tightening the vise of terror on the German Jews. She realized there was no future for a young Jewess in Germany, and she thought about escape. Hannah remembered her aunts and uncles who had gone to America to seek a new life. Perhaps a better life awaited her in America too.

Hannah wrote to Oma and Opa and told them of her plan. She asked for the address of Tanta Berta, Oma's sister in Oklahoma. Oma and Opa encouraged her to try her luck; they feared for their children's safety and wanted them all to escape from Germany. As soon as she got the address, Hannah fired off a letter to her aunt, pleading for sponsorship so she could join the family in America.

Hannah eagerly awaited a reply. When a letter came from America, she tore it open with anticipation. Was this her ticket to freedom? Could she escape the prison of life under the Nazis?

As she read Tanta Berta's response, Hannah's face fell.

Tanta Berta wrote that her family was unable to sponsor anyone at that time. Perhaps Tanta didn't realize the peril for a young Jewess in Germany, or perhaps her family was too poor to take in another person. Whatever the case, her refusal tragically changed the face of Hannah's history. She would have to remain in Germany, a victim of Hitler's devilish whims.

Instead of escaping from the Nazis, Hannah moved to Frankfurt, still cooking and keeping house for a Jewish family. She kept in close contact with Oma and Opa, and learned that her half-brother Simon, the oldest child, wanted to attend a Jewish trade school. She convinced her employer to allow Simon to board with them.

It was 1935, and Jews could no longer enroll in public schools. Germany had passed the Nuremberg laws, strict rules governing Jewish behavior, "for the protection of German blood and honor."

Hannah was glad to have the company of her brother as an anchor in the rough seas that buffeted the Jews of Frankfurt. Every day seemed to bring new rules that limited their freedom and their mobility.

One day Simon's trade school asked for volunteers to go to Palestine. They had two openings, and Simon quickly signed up. He wished he could take his sister Hannah along, but it was impossible. Only trade school students were permitted to apply.

Hannah bid her brother a tearful farewell and continued with her housekeeping duties. Her drab life was brightened by the friendship of the man who delivered meat to the household, Julius Cahn, twelve years her senior. Julius, a tall, handsome, blue-eyed Jewish butcher, was the fifth-born of Caroline and Heymann Cahn's eight children.

Enveloped in a world of hate, Julius and Hannah fell in love. Hannah wrote to Oma and Opa, telling them of her love and her plans for marriage. Oma objected strongly, but Hannah was not to be dissuaded. She and Julius married and moved to Mannheim to start a new life. Julius miraculously found work as a butcher, and they rented a small, one-bedroom apartment along the Rhein River.

Meanwhile, Nuremberg decrees continued to restrict Jewish life. By the summer of 1936, Jews were prohibited from so many jobs that almost half of German Jews couldn't get work. Jews were banned from practicing law, medicine or business.

By 1938, Jewish mothers found it difficult to buy milk for their babies. Many grocery stores, pharmacies and dairies bore the sign, "Jews Not Admitted."

This was the world into which I was born on March 29, 1938, the first child of Julius and Johanna Plaut Cahn.

I was still an infant on November 9, 1938, when gangs of Hitler's followers terrorized the streets, beating and killing Jews, destroying homes and stores, and smashing thousands of windows. Later known as Kristallnacht, it marked the violent beginning of Hitler's scheme to annihilate the Jewish people.

My parents sensed the danger and knew they had to get out of their apartment and hide. They quickly packed some sandwiches, bundled me in my buggy and rushed from the house. They dashed below street level to the path along the banks of the Rhein, praying they could find safety in the darkness.

They huddled close together to protect themselves from the chill of the wind and the icy fingers of fear that gripped their chests. My mother's hands trembled as she bent over the buggy, tucking the blanket carefully around my face.

The sounds of destruction punctuated the air on the street above. The clatter of splintering glass drew hoots and hollers from the blood-thirsty thugs. Shouts of encouragement shattered the rare moments of silence as the vandals prodded each other to commit yet more acts of devastation.

An occasional scream rang out on the streets, bringing terror to Hannah's heart, and she grasped Julius' hand tighter as they continued their aimless pacing. Their mouths were dry with the taste of fright as they tried to choke down the sandwiches they had packed.

My parents marched back and forth along the river for hours. When one of them stumbled with weariness, the other whispered words of encouragement. They kept my buggy in constant motion to lull me into the sleep of innocent bliss. Their greatest fear was that I would begin to howl and reveal the secret of our hidden existence.

Erich, like the pigeons he so intently observed, was still free in this photo taken in Mannheim prior to 1940.

Their interlocked hands turned blue with cold, and my parents yearned to return to the warmth of their apartment. They began to fear the vandals would never tire of prowling the streets.

After what seemed like an eternity, the sounds of the thugs evaporated. My parents waited a bit longer to make sure the coast was clear. They were unprepared for what they saw as they ascended to street level. Their path was littered with the rubble of hatred. They were barely able to walk as they sneaked back to the apartment. Under the Rhein River's blanket of protection, we had narrowly escaped the atrocities of Kristallnacht.

The next day my parents learned the full horror of what had transpired the night before. The winds of destruction had blown throughout Germany, and many Jews had been ripped from their homes. My mother feared the worst for Oma and Opa in Obervorschutz. There was no way to know their fate without visiting.

Hannah couldn't rest until she saw Oma. She told Vater she was leaving and hurriedly packed a few things. With baby Erich in tow, she dashed to the train station and headed for home.

The Adler household was in ruins when my mother and I arrived. Opa had been beaten, arrested and deported to the concentration camp at Buchenwalde. The family home had been ransacked, Opa's library confiscated, and three rooms upstairs seized by the Nazis. Oma was alone at home with her two youngest, ages six and one, and she was tormented with worry.

Oma wired her daughter Molly, my mother's half-sister, who was working in Frankfurt, to come home immediately. Simon was sheltered in Palestine; sons Eddie and Willy had been sent to an orphanage in Amsterdam for safekeeping. Oma paced the floors each night, not knowing what had become of Opa or how the family would survive without him.

Then the family's luck changed dramatically. First, a telegram came from Tanta Berta in Oklahoma. This time, perhaps awakened by the alarm of Kristallnacht, she was eager to help the family escape to the United States. She could sponsor one family — Oma, Opa, Molly, the boys and the babies. But it was too late for my mother, now married with a child of her own.

. The town burgermeister, a family friend, also came to Oma's rescue. Opa had served admirably for the Germans in World War I, receiving the Iron Cross for bravery. The burgermeister asked Oma to give him the Iron Cross and the telegram from America. He told her it was the best prospect for freeing Opa. Oma feared letting the cherished documents out of her sight, but she didn't know what else to do. She handed over the precious possessions and waited. Six weeks passed. Then Opa

*Vater Julius, already marked by the armband required
of all Jews, followed Erich's gaze skyward as they stole
a moment of play in a somber world.*

arrived home in the middle of the night, materializing like a
dream out of the darkness.

Opa immediately went to work, struggling to bind the
pieces of his broken spirit and negotiate for the family's exodus
to the United States.

The Adlers joined the masses of Jews seeking emigration,
but the Germans refused to issue them a quota number, that
priceless document required before one was permitted to leave
the country. In a last-ditch attempt at survival, Opa found a
loophole. He had been born in Antwerp, Belgium, and he con-

vinced the Nazis to grant emigration under the Belgian quota. The family could go to America!

The family stopped in Mannheim before escaping from Germany in April 1939. Oma and Opa, Molly and the two youngest came up to our apartment to say goodbye. My mother, cradling me in her arms, trembled, and sobs racked her body.

"Why is Hannah crying like that?" Molly asked. She added, full of false hope, "Hannah will soon join us."

Oma and Opa stopped next in Amsterdam to visit their sons Eddie and Willie, who did not yet have visas. They made plans for the boys to join the family after Oma and Opa found a home in the States. Four months later, in August 1939, on one of the last ships of Jews to elude the Nazi horrors, Eddie and Willie set off for America. The Adler family settled in Pueblo, Colorado, while we remained trapped in Mannheim.

The paths of freedom continued to crumble for Jews. By November 1939, Jews could not walk nor drive through certain streets, squares, parks or buildings. We were barred from the-atres, concert halls, museums, sports grounds and pools. All Jew-ish men had to take on the name Israel, all women, Sarah.

My parents tried to maintain a sense of normalcy in their lives. They continued to take me for strolls along the Rhein River, to snatch moments of family pleasure captured in photos. In June 1940, my mother bore her second child, a daughter, Suzanne.

Four months later, in October 1940, all remnants of our normal life were destroyed. The Nazis searched the buildings of Mannheim for Jewish families. They pounded on our apartment door and demanded that we leave immediately. There was no time to pack our belongings.

The streets resounded with the cries of dazed men, women and children. All the Jews of Mannheim had been snatched from their homes and sent into the streets.

Hannah Plaut Cahn's arms encircled baby Erich as her eyes caressed him.
Little did she know how soon her son would be torn from her embrace.

My mother, father, infant sister and I were loaded on a
truck by armed thugs who shouted insults and commands.
Neighbors who weren't moving fast enough were prodded into
action by the butts of guns. Finally the trucks were packed with
their human cargo.

The convoy rumbled through the streets of Mannheim,
carrying their heavy burden of anguished Jews. When the trucks
arrived at the train station, they came to an abrupt halt. The
soldiers ordered us off the trucks and pushed us into freight cars
designed to transport cattle.

We were crammed together, fighting for air, with no food, no
light and no knowledge of our destination. My parents fought back
the pressing crowds and gnawing panic to protect their infant

daughter and toddler son. The prisoners cried, screamed and tore at their hair and clothing with the insanity borne of terror. The air in the freight car turned foul with the smell of fear and urine.

We arrived at the Nazi holding camp of Gurs in the French Pyrenees after a couple of days of imprisonment in the freight cars. Gurs was the first and one of the largest detention camps in France, a place where Hitler warehoused German Jews until he arrived at the "final solution."

When we arrived, together with all Jews from Wurtemberg, Baden and Pfalz, there were 13,200 adults and 400 children in the camp. The cattle car doors were unsealed, and we staggered out, squinting as our eyes tried to adjust to the bright sunlight. The bodies of those who hadn't survived the trip tumbled from the train as the living pushed them out of the way.

Our family was separated; Vater was sent to the men's barracks, and my mother, sister and I were directed to the women's. At first, we had no beds, no straw mattresses, not even spoons or knives for our food. Clean drinking water was as scarce as toilet facilities as we fought for survival. Hundreds of our fellow inmates died of typhoid fever and dysentery during that first winter.

While the men and women were quartered in different "ilots" or sections, Vater could visit us during the day. My mother was served less than 800 calories of food each day, yet she miraculously managed to scrounge enough to keep her two babies alive.

Soon the camp management was taken over by civilians rather than the military, and conditions improved slightly. Cultural activities thrived despite the harsh conditions of the camp, and my parents could attend concerts, Hebrew classes and religious services. The Nazis, in a rare act of humanity, allowed nurses from Oeuvre de Secours aux Enfants (OSE), into the camp to care for the children. The nurses quickly realized that only removing the children from the camp would ensure their survival. Some children were smuggled out. In other cases, the OSE nurses removed the children under false pretenses, telling the Nazis that the youngsters required outside medical treatment. Still other children were removed, during a rare time of leniency, with the Nazis' permission.

But this apparent kindness was instead a clever, cruel Nazi trick. The Gestapo watched with sadistic amusement as frantic mothers clutched their babies to their breasts and weighed their fate. The choice tore some mothers asunder. Many jumped to their deaths from the barrack windows as their children disappeared from sight in the arms of French nurses.

On August 6, 1942, the first group of Jewish prisoners — 6,000 men, women and children — were deported from Gurs to Auschwitz. The air of Camp Gurs became thick with panic as the prisoners sensed a new era of Nazi cruelty.

Finally, my mother had to decide. Should she send her children away and hope our lives as orphans would be better than life with her at Gurs? Or should she keep us within arms' reach? In her final act of love and hope for a better tomorrow, she agreed to have us smuggled from the camp. The French Resistance brought me to an OSE children's home in Chabannes, France, in late August 1942.

The Nazis removed my parents from Gurs and transported them to the German holding camp at Rivesaltes less than a month later. On September 14, they left Rivesaltes with 569 others; 201 of them were German Jews; some still had their children with them.

The next stop in this dark journey was the deportation point of Drancy, outside of Paris, where my parents joined Convoy 33. The convoy, with 1,003 Jews, 586 males and 407 females, left the Drancy train station at 8:55 a.m. on September 16, 1942. Destination: Auschwitz. A telex to Adolf Eichmann confirmed the prisoners were on their way.

Hannah with her family in pre-war Germany. From left, Hannah, her sister Molly, her mother (Oma), her grandfather (Oma's father), her brothers Simon and Eddie, and her step-father (Opa).

Hannah and Julius were sealed in a moving dungeon without food and water for two days. It reminded them of the freight car two years earlier when they struggled to protect the lives of their children. This time, they were traveling alone. They prayed that their children had met a better fate as the convoy sped from France to the small Polish town of Auschwitz.

When the trainload of dehumanized Jews arrived at Hitler's largest death camp, the Nazi guards and doctors met them at the railroad siding. The deportees of Convoy 33 straggled out of the dark train into the daylight, and the doctors scrutinized them. Those Jews who appeared strong and healthy — 147 women and 300 men — were sent to the right; they were allowed to live and perform unspeakable chores for the Nazis. Julius Cahn was among them.

The rest of Convoy 33 filed to the left, directly to the "bathhouses," surrounded by well-kept gardens with a border of flowers. Perhaps the orchestra of young female inmates played light opera that day as the men, women and children undressed for the showers.

The unsuspecting victims were told it was time for delousing, but they were stuffed like trash into the crematorium. The doors slammed shut and were sealed, as was the prisoners' fate. The signal was given, and the executioners poured the deadly chemical, Zyklon B, into the overhead vents.

The Gestapo gawked like voyeurs through glass portholes, and in just a few minutes the hydrogen cyanide crystals began their destruction. When no water came through the shower heads, a rising tide of panic flooded the "bathers." Noxious fumes wafted through the vents, and the Jews crammed toward the locked doors. They trampled each other to death in a last, desperate attempt for life.

When the Nazis were sure all the screaming and writhing had stopped, they opened the doors. Over 500 prisoners from Convoy 33 were dead inside the "baths." The murders had taken only twenty minutes. Jewish slaves were sent into the hell hole to remove the bodies. Johanna Plaut Cahn was among the dead.

It was September 18, 1942, and my mother's short, tragic life was over. So was my childhood.

Chapter Two

Save A Child, Save the World

The inscription at the Yad Vashem Holocaust memorial in Israel reads, "He who saves one life, it is as if he saves the whole world."

My greatest wish is some day to inscribe the name of the family that saved my world on that memorial at Yad Vashem, for certainly they deserve to be with the Righteous Among Nations.

One of the biggest holes in my life has been my inability to find the French Christian family who rescued me. A frightened, motherless, four-year-old Jew, I went from the danger of the orphanage where I was briefly sheltered to the safety of this kind family's basement. Hundreds of times I have tasted the sweetness of an imagined reunion with my rescuers. On countless occa-sions I have struggled to mentally script my speech of gratitude.

I have yearned to fill my brain with forgotten details rather than the endless questions: Why did they decide to risk their lives — and the lives of their own children — to shelter a stranger? How did I arrive at their home? How did they manage to stretch their meager rations to feed me? How did they create a feeling of safety in the basement while still warning me of the danger that lurked just outside my small window?

I hid in this kind family's basement from 1942 to 1944. My life was saved by the miracle of their humanity. But I was robbed of my childhood by having to hide, to be silent, still and solitary. At an age when most children are blithely exploring their world, I was confined to a barren room. At a time when children are nurtured by the security of a mother's arms, I had only the protection of four colorless walls. While most children can be noisy with reckless abandon, my life depended on the mastery of silence.

The basement window, my only source of light, was the centerpiece of my survival. It signaled when to rise, when to sleep and when to despair. At daybreak, the sun streamed through the two-foot window, and I rolled off my hard, narrow cot to face another day alone. After washing in my little bath-room, I grabbed my well-worn clothes from a small chest and dressed. I glanced at my reflection in the mirror, half-heartedly combing my brown locks. Then I sat down on the edge of the bed and awaited my meal.

Upstairs, the house suddenly came alive with the muffled sounds of children's voices as the son and daughter, about my age, greeted the day. Although they were but a flight above me, their laughter seemed light years away. Playing with them was an impossible dream. The parents lived in fear that the Nazis might search the house at any time, and they kept me safely entombed down below.

I sat quietly on the bed, the hunger in my tummy echoed by the hunger in my heart. I heard a key turning in a lock, followed by the creak of the cellar door as it slowly opened. I perked up as the French woman's heels clicked down the wooden steps. I raced to the bottom of the steps and smiled as she descended deliberately toward me, balancing my breakfast tray.

"Good morning, Erich," she said softly in French. "I hope you had a good night."

I had learned the rudiments of French in her home, and I answered politely. "I slept fine, thank you."

She set the tray on my small table and turned back to the wooden stairs. She was disinclined to stay too long lest she create suspicion among the children upstairs who were impatiently waiting for their breakfast. I was never allowed to eat my meals with them; it was too risky.

As the basement door closed firmly behind my caretaker, so did my moments of happiness. Only the sounds of my spoon against the cereal bowl broke the hush. I was accustomed to the starvation diet of Gurs, and I quickly filled my stomach with the meager rations, but I couldn't fill the emptiness of my soul.

Quietly I cried for my mother, wishing with all my might that she would come and rescue me. The tears streamed down my face, and I shifted to the edge of my bed and waited for her. When the solitude overwhelmed me, I curled up in a ball, gathered my blanket around my neck and sought refuge in sleep. Napping intermittently helped to pass the endless day.

Even in sleep I listened for the scrape of the cellar door and the cautious footsteps descending. The symphony of sympathetic sounds awakened me, and I jumped off the cot to greet my visitor. As she placed lunch on my table, the French woman peered into my tear-stained face. Without asking any questions, she understood my pain and comforted me.

"It will not always be like this Erich. The bad men will go away some day, and you will not have to stay in the basement any more. Your family will come for you," she assured me. She put her arm around me and squeezed my thin shoulders before heading back up the stairs. Her hope was a ray of light in my darkened room. Three or four times a day, she brightened my life with her presence.

Her visits were always too short. The rest of the day I was completely alone, with only a few old toys and dogeared picture books for company.

When I finished my lunch, I half-heartedly picked up the small metal truck with peeling yellow paint. I sat down on the cold concrete floor and pushed the truck along the road I had invented along the cracks in the cement. The monotony of the path soon mirrored the boredom of my existence, and I sought new routes. I rode the well-used toy up the wall, standing on my cot and stretching my arm to bring the truck to new heights. Then I let it go. The truck careened wildly down the wall, crashed into the metal leg of my cot and rolled under the bed, disappearing into darkness as my parents had.

I nervously crawled into the black hole under the cot. My fingers tentatively roved around the dark crevices, seeking out the toy. I found dust balls and crumbs of forgotten food. Finally, I touched the cold metal of the truck. I grabbed it, backed quickly out of the darkness and resumed the truck's journey along the well-traveled cracks on the floor.

When I grew weary of my yellow truck, I sat on the edge of the cot and looked at the picture books. Soon I knew each page by heart. I was learning to read French without realizing it. I sometimes read the books backwards, or turned them upside down and giggled at the strangeness of the images.

I was always half-listening for the creak of the cellar door no matter how involved I was in my games. Hundreds of times each day I raced to the bottom of the stairs, thinking I had heard the door opening.

I invented a wishing game. I told myself that if I sat on the bed and looked at every picture in the book without jumping up to look for my visitor, the French woman would come back. Or better yet, the cellar door would open and my mother would magically appear before me.

My wish for the French woman came true when my timing was right. But the door never opened on my mother.

The image of my mother's face grew dimmer with each passing day. I sat on the edge of my cot, closed my eyes, squeezed them tight, and tried to recall the color of my mother's eyes and hair. But when I tried to see her in my mind's eye, her features became a blur, melding with those of my French caretaker. I couldn't remember my mother!

My mother's face — the face I had discovered as a nursing infant, the face I had tentatively explored with my pudgy baby fingers, the face that had smiled down on me as I attempted my first steps — had vanished from my brain.

My eyes shot open, and I bolted off the cot. I paced the narrow room, wringing my hands and battling to escape from my torturous thoughts. Just as I could not flee the basement, neither could I dodge my terror. My breathing became shallow; panic permeated every pore of my frail body. I walked faster, but I couldn't shake off the cloak of anguish enveloping me.

Terrifying questions screamed from my soul though not a word escaped my throat. Why can't I picture my own mother's face? Where did she go? Will I ever see that face again?

The most horrifying notion shot like a bullet through my mind: What if she finally comes to rescue me and I don't know her? The thought was more than I could bear. I crumbled on the cot and sobbed into my hands, the saltwater tears mixing with the fear-induced sweat.

When the last glimmer of light disappeared from the window, I settled down for the night. We were unable to risk a lamp or even a candle, so when darkness fell, there was nothing to do but sleep. I lay down on my cot and pulled the thin covers up around my face. I closed my eyes and prayed that tomorrow my mother would come.

I fell asleep, wrapped in the blanket of the French family's charity. Most of the time I slept soundly until daybreak, and the tedious pattern of my days was repeated.

The French woman would visit me only once or twice on days when the danger of discovery was heightened by the presence of Nazis on the streets. It was then she firmly reminded me of the omnipresent menace.

"You must be quiet and still, Erich. There is great danger. You can see the bad men outside your window. If they see you, they will hurt you and my family upstairs," the woman warned.

Her caution shattered the tenuous sense of security that the hidden basement provided. Goose bumps covered my skinny arms as I grew cold with fear. I was answerable not only for my own survival, but also for the kind family's future. My bony shoulders sagged with the weight of my responsibilities, and I curled up on my bed, seeking to make myself even smaller and less conspicuous.

I was afraid to move. Even turning the pages of my picture book seemed too risky. What if I dropped the book? What if someone outside heard me cough or sneeze? I couldn't risk the danger. I stayed tightly curled in the fetal position on my cot. My hands fell asleep, and I got pins and needles in my legs from attempting to be still. My shoulder ached where it pressed into the rigid cot.

That evening, I heard marching up and down the streets outside my garden window. My curiosity overtook my fear, and I had to see what was happening. Slowly, I uncurled my body and sat up on the hard cot. I placed my right foot carefully on the floor, then slowly lowered my left foot next to it. I stood up and tiptoed to the window.

I cautiously got up on my stool and peeked out the window. Big, black, high leather boots filled my view. I shuddered as those shiny black feet marched only yards from my face. The soldiers laughed loudly as they swaggered by my window, and I cowered. If I made a sound, the men in the black boots would stomp into the house and snap the thin thread of our survival.

My teeth rattled with fear, and my heart pounded so loudly that I feared the soldiers would hear it. I turned around and slinked back to the cot.

I sought sanctuary under the covers, but I could not rest for long. I awoke with a start from a fitful sleep as loud noises shattered the silence. Gun shots rang out all around us, shredding my thin blanket of protection. I lay in the darkness for hours, my eyes wide with fear and my gaunt body shaking in terror. I hungered for the protection of my mother's arms, and my starvation created a huge, black hole inside.

I was much happier on the rare night when all was quiet in the streets. Then the French woman fetched me for a much-welcome journey upstairs.

"Come, Erich. It is safe tonight. Come outside for a few minutes," she said.

I slithered up the stairs like a snake making his first foray above ground. I stood silently just outside the front door, guarded by the darkness. The French woman and her husband stood by my side like two sentinels. Their eyes darted from left to right, up and down the empty street for the first portent of danger. I savored the gift of the gentle breeze caressing my face for just a few minutes. It was an uneasy peace, and I shortly had to return to the stifling safety of the cellar.

I can recall only one time that the father and children joined me in the basement. They descended into my cavern to celebrate a special occasion with me. It might have been my birthday, or perhaps it signaled liberation.

My solitary room was jammed with life and laughter for the first time, and I didn't know what to make of it.

"It's a celebration, take a puff of my cigar," the father joked, pushing the big, brown object with its smoldering tip toward my face. I was eager to join the frivolity, and I leaned forward. He placed the cigar against my lips, and I inhaled deeply. I sputtered and gasped as the sickening taste filled my mouth. The acrid smell invaded my nose, and I felt dizzy. I was lightheaded from the cigar and the rarity of companionship.

The liberation of France meant the liberation of Erich. Finally, after two years in hiding, I could break out of my underground home and wander freely without fear. But freedom had as little meaning to me as to a caged bird. I feared leaving the safety of my basement and the kindness of the French family. Life with them was all I could remember. I had forgotten my mother's face and what it was like to be enveloped in her arms. I had forgotten my home in Mannheim and had buried the memories of Gurs.

In six years of life, I had been uprooted four times: first leaving Mannheim, then Gurs, then the orphanage, and now the kind French family. Once again I was being sent off into the unknown.

Chapter Three

In Search of A Home

With liberation, the cellar doors and attic hatches were unlatched, and hundreds of Jewish children tumbled into freedom. Hitler's henchmen had murdered one-and-a-half million innocent youth, and the lucky survivors were now both orphaned and homeless.

Once again the Oeuvre de Secours (OSE) came to the rescue, setting up orphanages around France while working tirelessly to reunite the hidden children with surviving family members.

When I left my French Christian family in 1944, I was placed in the OSE children's home at Montintin. In August 1945, I was moved to the orphanage in Draveil. It was there, after three years away from family, I learned I was not alone in the world. I lay in the infirmary, feeling out of sorts one day, and the nurses brought a small, pretty, dark-haired girl to see me.

"This is your sister, Suzanne," they said. We stared blankly at each other.

"Who is this stranger?" I thought. I didn't remember any sister, and I felt nothing for her. I had learned to survive on my own; no other relationships endured.

Suzanne's story was one more testimony to human kindness. After leaving Gurs, she had been sheltered by an eighteen-year-old French woman who pretended the child was hers, raising her openly rather than keeping her in hiding.

I lived in the boy's dormitory at Draveil, and I rarely saw my sister. We did not seek each other out, but chatted politely in passing. The long, tedious days that marked life in the basement were replaced by days filled with regimented activities. We awoke early each morning and went to the large community bathroom to shower. After a hearty breakfast, we attended classes to make up for the lessons we had lost in our years of hiding. The orphanage offered us weekly Jewish services to reconnect us to our forgotten heritage.

We played in a large room filled with toys and dolls under the watchful eye of seamstresses who kept their hands busy sewing clothing for us. I had been alone for so long that I had no idea how to play with other children. I was uncoordinated, small and shy, so I tried to avoid the boisterous games that the boys played. When a ball came my way, I dodged it. The urchins soon guessed my weaknesses, and their taunts reverberated through my soul as these young war victims became my persecutors. The children in the playroom pounded my spirits with hurricane force, and I felt more alone than ever.

I was well-fed for the first time in years, but a great emptiness lingered in my soul. The busy nurses provided food, clothing and company, but had no time for hugs. My frail body still hungered for a mother's embrace.

The OSE's primary goal was to reunite families, and continuous detective work resulted in finding parents or other relatives who had survived Hitler's destruction. Each day, children streamed from the orphanage on the arms of mothers and fathers, aunts and uncles.

"Some day, someone will come for you, too," the caretakers promised me. Their sense of hope was the whisper of a promise — tomorrow will be better. I waited anxiously for my mother to come.

Indeed two separate efforts to find me were under way, and letters were being exchanged across the world. The first letter came from my great-uncle, Albert Nash, in Oklahoma in January 1945. Then on February 16, 1945, Opa wrote to the orphanage from Pueblo, Colorado: "Through the office of OSE in New York, I was informed that two grandchildren of mine, Erich Cahn and Suzanne Cahn, are in your care. I would like to hear from you more personal news from the children and how I can help direct. Could you inform me how I can get the children here to this country?"

The OSE, intent on protecting its young charges, hesitated to release us. The agency responded to Albert Nash on February 21. "They are beautiful children in very good health... The mother was deported, but the children hope and wait for her return. As they are still very young, perhaps it will be preferable to delay their emigration."

On March 28, the OSE wrote to its counterpart in New York, again asking that our emigration be delayed. "As the children are still very young, we think that it would be more advisable to wait until the end of the war before undertaking the various steps for their emigration to the U.S.A. As always, the best way to help these children is to send them clothing parcels and some sweets."

Opa continued to write, urging that Suzanne and I be sent to America. He must have pressed the point, because on October 19, the OSE sent him detailed instructions on how to get us to America. Before we could emigrate, the letter said, the OSE required his income tax returns, employers' certificates and statements of bank accounts to prove he could support us. And transportation was a problem.

"The main impediment in the way of speedy emigration of civilians to the United States is the lack of places on the ships which are reserved for the U.S. Forces. It is, however, quite possible that ... will be able to contract a ship in the beginning of next year, and we do advise you to reserve the places in advance,..." the OSE told Opa.

The OSE again assured Opa that we were doing well, but changed their outlook about where we should be. "You can be sure that your grandchildren are well attended to. They live in one of our children's homes where there are Jewish children only so you need not worry about this point. Of course, it would be much better if they could soon join their own family, but we must warn you that the passport formalities must take several months."

And then, on November 2, 1945, another letter came to the OSE. "The day nursery of Limoges, has transmitted to us a letter from Mr. Julius Cahn. Mr. Julius Cahn had been deported from Rivesaltes in 1942 and is actually in Leutesdorf on the Rhein River, 50 Haupstrasse. In 1942 he entrusted his two children: Erich and Suzanne Cahn to the day nursery of Limoges.... Could you tell us if you know where these two children are presently, and could you contact the father?..."

My father (Vater) was alive, one of only thirty-eight Jews from Convoy 33, with its 1,003 passengers, to survive Auschwitz!

On December 13, 1945, the OSE wrote to the Squadron Chief of Occupied Ludwigshafen, "We understand perfectly well Mr. Kahn's (sic) desire to see his children again, but we believe it would not be reasonable at this time to let the children undertake such a long trip to Germany, in view of their young age.

Perhaps, Mr. Kahn could obtain the necessary authorization to visit his children here. We could then decide together as to the future of the children."

The stream of letters from America and Germany continued into 1946. Opa sent all the paperwork to have us brought to America. He reported that his annual income was $2,000, and he had $5,000 in assets. But he was still unaware that my father had been found alive. Two great-aunts came to visit us at the orphanage, promising to bring us to America with them. That was not to be.

On July 2, 1946, the OSE wrote, "He (Julius Cahn) informed us of his wishes not to let the children go to America and we have stopped all emigration procedures. We do not know if the grandparents are aware of this."

Meanwhile, Vater was growing understandably impatient. He wrote a letter to the OSE, dated August 20, 1946: "You can probably understand that having been out of the concentration camp for a year and a quarter, I'd like to have my children back with me. I have already informed you that everything is ready for the children. I have a house with a yard and they will lack for nothing. For this reason, I urgently request that you send the papers for Suzanne and Erich Cahn to Draveil, and that as soon as possible you will entrust my little ones to someone who can bring them here?..."

The OSE wrote its final memo on September 9, 1946: "We advise you that: Cahn Erich and Cahn Suzanne who reside in our house of Draveil, left yesterday, September 8, for Germany in order to be reunited with their father, Mr. Julius Cahn, residing at 50 Hauptstrasse in Leutesdorf a/Rhein."

After six years in exile, we were headed back to Germany to be with Vater.

Chapter Four

Vater, the Stranger

Suzanne and I chattered in French as we hurried down the cobblestone streets of Leutesdorf to join our Vater. The cavernous hole inside my orphan's heart yearned to be filled with Vater's love. Vater walked briskly down the street toward us, and I silently prayed for his arms to surround me in greeting. Instead his icy blue eyes inspected me from what seemed like ten feet above. With the heightened senses of a survivor, I felt his disappointment in this small, shy son. The emptiness inside echoed with despair as I gazed up at this remote stranger who was my Vater.

A thin, stern woman stood like a soldier at attention in the doorway of our home. "This is Theresa, our housekeeper. She will take care of you and you must mind her," Vater said. My hopes for love plummeted as my eyes probed Theresa's face for the soft curves of maternal tenderness and found instead the rigid lines of a bitter old maid.

That first day, Suzanne and I bantered in French, the only language we knew. Theresa bristled at the sound of the enemy tongue.

"I will not have you talking about me in French," Theresa ordered. "You will speak only German in this house."

Like a black-booted soldier, Theresa immediately jolted me into fearful silence. She was taking my voice away. I knew no German; how could I communicate? But I had learned never to question authority. I had lived a regimented life in the orphanage, and in the French cellar my very survival had depended on blind obedience to adults. I knew it was futile to argue with Theresa, and Vater would grant no appeals. My only choice was to learn German quickly, and I never spoke French again.

Our two-story house on Hauptstrasse was comfortable, but as cold and forbidding as Vater. The living room, with its overstuffed couch and chairs, was a dark sepulcher. No family pictures nor even dime-store prints broke the monotony of its walls.

We soon settled into a routine. Vater enrolled us in the nearest school, de Katholic Volksschule zu Leutesdorf. A Catholic primary school that we attended year-round, it was about a mile from home, and we walked to school each morning. I studied reading, writing, arithmetic, music and German. We were the only Jewish family in town, and "Judisch," was marked prominently on the front page of my report card. I was excused from catechism and Bible study classes.

Vater expected good grades and like an eager young puppy, I complied. My quarterly report cards were filled with grades of "good" and "very good." Vater scrutinized the teacher's notes and signed with a flourish of his fountain pen but without a word of praise. To keep up my grades, I spent afternoons quietly studying in the sunlit bedroom I shared with my sister. Our room overlooked the street, and the clack of cars and horses across

Vater Julius Cahn, whose stern good looks intimidated Erich from the day they were reunited in Germany in 1946 until their final meeting in 1970.

the cobblestones provided diversion to the dull routine of my days. I switched on my lamp to finish up my work as day turned to night. Then I sat and waited patiently to be called downstairs for dinner.

Suzanne and I dined alone in silence on most nights. Theresa prepared and served our meal but did not sit down to eat with us. Vater, a shadowy presence in our lives, rarely ate at

*A photo of Erich taken in the orphanage at Draveil
after the war. Almost 50 years later, another
child survivor of the Holocaust shared her copy
of the identical picture at the
Hidden Child Conference.*

home. His coal business took him to Cologne and other neighboring cities, and he often stayed away overnight, leaving us in Theresa's capable but cold hands. An efficient robot, she provided us with a well-run house, but not a loving home.

My prayers for hugs went unanswered. Even when Vater was at home, he faded into the background. Vater seemed incapable of expressing any affection, and I didn't understand. A needy eight year old, I thought only about my own aching soul and not about his longings.

When Vater greeted me each day, did he see a portrait of my mother's face and feel the pain of her absence? I could not know because he never uttered Hannah's name nor spoke of their life together. Not once did he share a photo of Hannah or the family. Nor did Vater ever speak of the horrors he must have endured to survive the Nazi's most evil death camp. He buried the past in a hole as deep as the cavern of need in my heart.

I grasped nothing about Vater's life during the four years we were separated and how that might have affected him. I didn't know about the loss of his own siblings: a brother butchered in Bergen Belsen and a sister annihilated in Auschwitz. I didn't know that three of his siblings barely had escaped the Nazi terrors by fleeing abroad. I didn't know that his only siblings remaining in Germany, two sisters, escaped the Nazi terrors by marrying Christians.

In my child's orb of ignorance and vanity, I thought Vater's remoteness somehow reflected his disappointment in me. I was so different from him. While he had the vitality of a man who labored outdoors, I was as puny as a bookworm. While he was a leader among the townspeople, I had trouble making friends. The games that came naturally to my classmates were as foreign as the German language to me.

Theresa brought her nephew, Boob, to our home to provide me with a playmate. Vater warmed instantly to the outgoing, athletic Boob. I paled by comparison. "If I were only more like Boob," I thought. "Maybe then Vater would love me."

I was not the only one pursuing Vater's affection in vain. Theresa wanted love too. Vater saw her simply as housekeeper and nanny, but she dreamed of a deeper relationship. So Vater's philandering wounded us all.

I quickly learned the telltale signs though I never saw one of his women. Vater's bedroom was next to ours, and he generally rose first. On some weekend mornings, however, his door remained tightly shut. He had brought a woman home the night before. I tiptoed down the stairs on those days, trying in vain to please Theresa. It was futile. Theresa, with the bitterness of a rejected old maid, hurled her disappointment at me.

We bathed only on Saturday nights and on the Christian holidays that we celebrated with Theresa. She dragged the big metal washtub into the center of the kitchen on Christmas Eve. Water, hauled in from the backyard pump, was heated on the coal stove to fill the tub. Then Theresa left me in privacy to take my bath and get in my pajamas.

Freshly scrubbed, we snuggled around the Christmas tree and turned the lights low. A fearsome rattling of chains outside startled me, and I ran for cover. I shivered in the corner, caught in a stranglehold of fear, until the nerve-wracking noise ceased as suddenly as it had started. Theresa, uncharacteristically cheerful, proclaimed that St. Nicholas had come with gifts. Unwanted memories of noisy German soldiers outside the basement window crowded my mind, leaving no room for the joy of Christmas.

St. Nicholas brought Suzanne a dollhouse, decorated with five tiny bottles filled with red, green and gold granules. A few days later, Vater and Theresa left us at home alone. The colored granules looked delicious, and my ripening sweet tooth couldn't endure the temptation. I seized this reprieve from Theresa's perpetually vigilant eyes.

"Please, Suzanne, let me open one bottle. It won't hurt anything," I begged. She was hesitant at first, but finally surrendered to my pleas. I snatched the bottle with red candy and carried it into the kitchen like a thief escaping with his booty. I yanked at the top of the bottle, and it shattered in my hand, spilling candy all over the kitchen floor. I tasted some, but its delicious flavor couldn't quash the rising bile of fear in my stomach.

"Now look what you've done," I thought. "They will really get me for this." My heart raced as I pushed the broom around the kitchen floor, sweeping up each grain of evidence like a seasoned criminal. But I had no way to replace the shattered bottle, so I couldn't hide my crime from Theresa. She quickly assessed the situation when she returned home and determined the culprit. Theresa spat cruel words while I bowed with shame.

I stewed in a pot of self-pity, and my shame turned to anger. What's the big deal about a little glass bottle? Why are they so quick to judge and so slow to love? The cavern inside grew larger, and I withdrew deeper into it.

Our house was dark and cold, but the world outside was lush and exciting, filling my heart with hope for tomorrow. Each season brought a different adventure. In springtime, Suzanne and I would hike up the hill behind our house and tromp through the woods and meadows, filling our wooden baskets with wildflowers. All of Leutesdorf joined us, and soon hundreds of baskets brimmed with a riot of red, yellow and purple. When our baskets were filled, we'd return to town, tossing our flowers on the road until the cobblestones became a patchwork quilt of vibrant color, and the air smelled like fine perfume. It was like a promise for a better life.

Earlier in the spring the cobblestones were covered not by flowers but by water. Spring runoff meant the Rhein River would gush over its banks, flooding the lower end of town and creating a children's sea of fun. Instead of riding in Vater's unreliable old truck, we could travel in style, rowing boats through the waterlogged streets.

In winter, my Christmas sled became the favored mode of transport. The long, steep hill behind our house provided the perfect place to slide, and when we got cold we could huddle around the coal stove in the kitchen.

Erich as a boy in Leutesdorf, where he lived with his austere father and a reproachful housekeeper after the war.

The best time of year outdoors was fall — grape-picking season in Vater's vineyard. I'd trek up the sledding slope every afternoon after school and each weekend. I climbed the steep road and journeyed three miles into the woods. I crested the hill and spotted the vines laden with thousands of ripe grapes, lined up along metal fences like eager ingenues prime for the picking. I could hardly wait to feel the soft, smooth green grapes in my hands. I grabbed and gobbled a bunch of grapes, savoring their juicy sweetness. Vater was generous, and I could eat until my tummy was as swollen as the vines while I filled the wooden bushel baskets.

I was surrounded by townspeople, children and adults who picked and ate the succulent fruit. The sun warmed my body, and the gossiping laborers warmed my heart as I felt a rare sense of camaraderie. When I filled the first basket, I dragged it over to Vater's pickup truck, lifted it inside, and picked up another empty bushel.

Finally the old pickup truck was lined with baskets cascading with grapes. We continued laboring, filling an endless supply of baskets as Vater's driver descended with the fruits of our labor and dumped the grapes into huge wooden vats behind the house. The vat was cranked, and juice poured out the spout on the bottom, leaving stems and skins behind. The driver headed up the hill for the next batch of bushels while the men below cleaned and readied the vats. The freshly squeezed grape juice was poured into fermentation barrels and hauled down the steps to our wine cellar, a deep cave under the house.

How I remember that cellar! One spring day, I was lying on my bed and discovering my body. Vater came looking for me, and hearing no answer, burst into the room without knocking. When he realized I was masturbating, he glared at me, his blue eyes turning to ice.

"What are you doing, Erich? I will teach you a lesson so that you will never do this again," Vater shouted. He jostled me down the stairs and outside the kitchen door. He lifted the heavy double doors to the wine cellar and shoved me inside.

"You will stay in here until I come to get you," Vater commanded.

The doors slammed shut with deathly finality, and I was alone in the dank dungeon. My eyes strained to adjust to the darkness, and I sighed with relief at escaping from Vater's fury. The minutes turned to hours, and I began to wonder when Vater would come back to get me. I considered sneaking up the stairs and prying open the door. But I was paralyzed by fear. I thought Vater had forgotten me, and I was destined to live out my life in a cellar. I crumbled to the earthen floor and sobbed as the dim afternoon light that peeked through the cracks of the cellar door faded into evening's darkness.

I cried myself to sleep after several hours in the blackness, with only empty wine vats for company. I awoke with bones aching from the dampness of my underground prison, and I struggled to control my bowels. "Will Vater ever come for me, or must I live alone in a basement once again?" I wondered, burrowed in a cave of loneliness.

Finally, I saw daylight peering through the cracks in the door, and I heard heavy footsteps approaching outside. Vater thrust open the doors and ordered me out. I was blinded by the brightness of the sun and the darkness of my hatred. I stumbled up the cellar stairs to be stricken with more angry words.

"Do not tell your sister why you were punished, Erich. If she asks, tell her you were punished for lying," Vater warned. "And never do that filthy thing again."

Grapes, kept in the cellar for weeks, sweetened into wine. A pubescent boy, abandoned in the same cellar overnight, turned sour. My relationship with Vater, never having fully ripened, now totally decayed. I had vowed in the blackness of the wine cellar that Vater never would hurt me again. I would stop trying to fill my emptiness with his love.

Before my night in the cellar, I resented Vater's trips away from home, each one further proof of rejection. Now I wanted him gone. I preferred Theresa's uncaring coolness to Vater's hot temper.

Vater suddenly changed a couple of years later. He had treated idle conversation as a fine jewel, to be bestowed frugally. Now he became downright gabby, telling us fairy tales about America. He spun stories of a land filled with promise and happiness where all the people were rich, and life was easy. I listened with bored politeness until one day he broke the news.

"Erich, you and Suzanne are going to America to live with your grandparents. It will be a better life," he told me. He said he couldn't leave his business, and he would stay behind.

As much as I dreaded his anger, fear echoed through the chasms of my soul at the thought of leaving Vater for an unknown family across the sea. Why did Vater decide to send away the only children he would ever have? Perhaps he truly believed life would be better in America, and we deserved the chance. Maybe he was weary of the burdens of single parenthood. Possibly he could no longer endure the painful memories that we evoked. I never knew the real reason, so I could only imagine the worst. I was certain it was my failure as a son that led to our separation.

Ironically, the one time I earned Vater's respect came after the decision to send us to America. I had wanted to prove myself worthy of Vater's love for years, and now it was too late.

Vater tested my mettle on a warm spring day in 1949. "Erich, you are old enough to start doing errands. I want you to go to Koblenz and pick up some important documents for your trip to America," Vater said.

With the precision of a scientist, he painstakingly recorded the route. My hand trembled as I reached for the instructions. Koblenz seemed light years away though it was only twenty-five miles from home. Could I master the challenge and accomplish the mission?

Vater gave me permission to miss school, but I rose early anyway and dressed in my school clothes. I was bolstered by a pocketful of marks and a head full of determination when I strode down the cobblestone streets toward the train station.

I dug into my pocket, carefully counted the coins and reached up to the station master's window to purchase a roundtrip ticket to Koblenz. I entered the train and plopped down near the window as the tension oozed from my pores. I gave a sigh of relief as I peered out the window, watching the coal cargo boats wind along the Rhein. I had jumped the first hurdle in the race to please Vater.

The train stopped first at Neuwied, a town slightly larger than Leutesdorf. I knew that I should remain on the train and waited patiently until it jerked back into motion toward my destination.

We arrived at the Koblenz station just a few minutes later. The station looked like a swarming anthill. Hundreds of people marched with certainty in all directions, and I felt lost in the maze of activity. My mission outstripped my shyness, and I looked up at the first approachable face.

"Please, can you tell me how to get to the government building?" I whispered. The man pointed me in the right direction, and I headed out of the station on the final leg of my journey. I stopped twice along the way to confirm directions with self-assured adults walking by me.

The train station in Leutesdorf, Germany, in a photo taken by Jeff Cahn in 1990.

The granite government building loomed in front of me after a twenty-minute walk. Fortified by my success, I yanked at the large wooden doors. My footsteps echoed as I stepped into the bowels of the entryway. I peered into the first office, asked for help and was directed to the second floor. I marched up the stone steps and into the emigration office, pulled Vater's note from my pocket and handed it to the woman behind the counter. She glanced at the note and disappeared into the back office, returning with a distinguished gentleman who instructed me to sit down and wait. The official returned in a few minutes and presented me with the gift of a brown manila envelope.

I clasped the envelope to my chest like a life preserver and walked out of the government building with a smile on my face. I had gotten the papers. I headed confidently back to the train station, retracing my steps without stopping to ask for directions.

My confidence wavered as I entered the vast station. A choice of six platforms confused me, and I finally had to ask which train would take me back to Leutesdorf. Although the train would not leave for two hours, I was too anxious to explore. I settled down on a wooden bench to wait, still clasping the envelope to my heart. My whole body shimmered with a feeling of success.

Finally, the train to Leutesdorf arrived, and I boarded with the impatience of a travel-weary soldier. I stared out the train windows, wishing away the moments until my reunion with Vater.

I rushed off the train at the Leutesdorf station and dashed down the cobblestone streets, clutching my treasure. Vater was waiting for me. I flushed with excitement while I handed him the package and jabbered about my trip. He painstakingly opened the envelope and scrutinized its contents. Then he looked down at me.

"You have done a good job Erich. Tonight, I will give you money to go to the carnival," Vater said.

I felt a hundred feet tall and the hollow of my soul filled with pride. I was inflated with self-esteem when I floated down to the carnival by the Rhein. I jumped on the carousel, gobbled an ice cream and played some carnival games as I relished my success. I savored the sounds and smells of the city I would soon be leaving.

But my success with Vater had come too late. My fate was already sealed, and soon I would be exiled to a foreign land and a foreign language for the third time in my short life.

Chapter Five

Journey to the Promised Land

I waited with anticipation for months. Everything stayed the same on the surface. I remained tied to the daily routine of school, chores and homework. But deep inside, my spirit flew free as I began unknotting the ropes of Vater's bondage.

Finally, one day in late April, Vater said, "Erich, the paperwork is now complete. Tomorrow, I will take you to Munich, and you will begin your journey to America."

That evening, buoyed by my hopes of a better tomorrow, I stuffed my paltry possessions into a small cardboard suitcase. A few toys, my short pants, some button-down shirts and a sweater or two filled the box. I had no photos to remind me of the past, and I could hardly wait for the new light of morning and my escape from the darkness of Leutesdorf.

I woke with a sense of expectation. I dressed in short navy pants and a wool sweater and bent to tie my only pair of shoes. My blue eyes, clear of any tears of regret, looked around the cold bedroom for the last time. I smiled to myself as I thought about being free from the disapproving stare of Vater's icy blue eyes. I clutched my suitcase to my breast and hurried down the stairs, ready for an adventure.

Theresa was nowhere in sight as we closed the front door on a chapter in our lives. Suzanne, Vater and I piled in the cab of his two-ton truck and rumbled down the cobblestone street to the train station.

Suffused with happy memories of my earlier train trip to Koblenz for Vater, I boarded the train eagerly and settled in a window seat. Once again I could watch the barges float along the Rhein. My mind flowed as freely as the river in its journey to new lands. My spirits soared as the train put distance between me and Leutesdorf.

The monotonous clacking of the train was echoed by Vater's upbeat monologue. "Life in America will be very good for you. Everyone is rich there. You will be happy in America," Vater assured us again and again.

We arrived in Munich in what seemed like no time at all. There Vater beckoned a taxi that took us to a large way station for displaced children. The gray stone buildings filled most of a city block. I was taken to the one-story boys' dormitory where I was assigned to an iron cot. The cots, lined up like soldiers in the enormous room, each belonged to a boy between the age of eight and fourteen who would spend a few days at the way station on his journey to a new home. The monotony of the institutional white walls was broken by an occasional window overlooking the street where I could watch the traffic ride slowly by.

Vater quickly and efficiently got us settled in our rooms. He seemed eager to leave. Four years earlier when we had reunited, my heart was filled with the hope of being wrapped in a blanket of warm hugs. Now, I expected nothing. And Vater gave nothing. Not one hug nor kiss of farewell shattered the four-year record of tactile neglect.

"Goodbye and good luck in America. You will be happy there," Vater said casually. He was as indifferent as if I were leaving for school for the day, not crossing an ocean to begin a new life. We turned from each other, and I felt the burden of his disapproval lift from my shoulders. I was ready to start anew in America.

My patience was to be tested once again. Physical exams, inoculations and more paperwork delayed our departure. I ran around the dirt yard of the institution with the other children for a week, biding the time until I could get on with my voyage. I lay on my iron cot each night, closed my eyes and conjured up images of life in the promised land.

The days and nights passed slowly, but finally it was time to get on with our journey. Once again, Suzanne and I gathered up our belongings in our tattered suitcases and headed for a new home. The driver came around with his car, and Suzanne, I and a woman from the home bundled aboard, headed for the Munich airport.

It was a warm spring day, and the gentle breeze caressed our faces as we mounted the metal steps into the belly of the two-engine plane. The stewardess escorted us to the middle of the plane where there were four seats across. Suzanne settled down in the window seat while I sat next to her at the aisle.

The engine roared, the plane rattled, and soon we were airborne. My spirits flew with the mechanical bird's ascent, and I chattered gaily to Suzanne about our new life. I had to shout to be heard over the engine's roar, and soon we quieted down, both lost in our own thoughts.

We were landing in Copenhagen before I knew it. I stretched to look over Suzanne and out the window, and I was amazed by the imposing beauty of the city. We walked down the metal staircase into the late afternoon sunshine, and both my body and soul drank up the warmth. I was filled with a sense of well-being.

Suzanne and I, the only two unaccompanied children on the plane, followed the other passengers into the terminal. A social worker in her late thirties met us as we entered the building.

She spoke to us in German. "You will be in this airport for a few hours before you get on the next plane. I will take you to dinner."

We chatted as we ate, and we meandered around the airport grounds to pass the time. The airport was clean, much newer than the one in Munich, and seemed like a very friendly place. The hours passed quickly as we soaked in the beauty of the city and watched the planes as they taxied in and out of the airport.

When our departure time arrived, the social worker walked us out of the terminal and up the metal stairs onto our second plane. This was a bigger model, with four engines, for our journey across the Atlantic. It was my turn to get a window seat, and I peered out the porthole with anticipation as we left the beautiful city of Copenhagen behind.

It was 5:30 in the evening, and as we flew, the sky glowed with the reds and oranges of sunset. The water below and the fiery sky surrounding us took my breath away, and I gasped with awe. Too soon, the light show was over, and night began to fall. As the sky darkened, so did my mood.

Suddenly I was gripped with fear. I realized that although our home in Leutesdorf had the warmth of an iceberg, I had learned to navigate around it. Now I was headed into uncharted waters. I struggled to submerge the advancing tide of terror. In the privacy afforded by the darkness of the night and the roar of the engines, I turned to the window and sobbed.

I felt trapped between the darkness of the black ocean and the ebony sky as my misty eyes peered out the window. Memories of solitude brought a steady flow of tears. I cried as I recalled other dark nights: the French basement during blackout and the Leutesdorf wine cellar during my punishment. A wail escaped my lips as I was pierced by the irrefutable truth that man is a solitary traveler in this world. I had never felt more forsaken.

Unanswered questions filled me with anxiety: Who are these grandparents in America? What will life be like for me? How will I communicate? What are the children like? Will they make fun of me with my German accent?

Awash in a sea of tears, I finally fell into a fitful sleep. I awoke to our landing in Newfoundland. The airport was shrouded in a thick mist, and the workers outside huddled against the wind. The change in weather matched my shift in mood. Where Copenhagen had been sunny and welcoming, Newfoundland was frigid and foreboding.

Our plane was refueled immediately, and we pushed through the haze to the runway. My heart sank under the weight of sadness as the plane ascended toward our final destiny. I dozed fitfully, my body and mind struggling to overcome the bruises of the journey.

When I awoke, I could see dawn-lit land breaking the monotony of the endless black sea. I pressed my nose against the small window and gaped at the aerial view of the New York skyline.

The tall buildings jutted out of the ground, their long arms like fate reaching to pull our plane out of the sky.

America, I thought. So this is America. The majestic sight was etched in my memory. But I felt nothing. I was no longer sad, but I wasn't excited. I was just numb. The deluge of emotion during the long, lonely journey had drained all my energy. I waited passively to see what fate would bring next.

Suzanne and I filed off the plane like robots. Yet another nameless, nondescript social worker met us at the terminal. She hurried us into a waiting car. We drove past endless rows of brick apartment buildings, but I got no glimpse of the impressive New York skyline that I had viewed from the air. Soon we arrived at one more stark, gray orphanage where immigrants like us were housed until our American sponsors could cut through the endless rolls of red tape. I had long ago grown accustomed to making every stop my home, and I unpacked my few belongings and placed them in the small dresser drawers assigned to me.

We had a great surprise the next day. Suzanne and I were called to the reception area and told we had visitors. A short man with dark curly hair greeted us warmly in German. It was my mother's brother Simon, who had escaped the Nazis by volunteering in Palestine. His wife, Esther, a pretty woman dressed in a skirt and blouse, stood at his side. They were living in New York, and they had come to see us.

Suzanne and I took them on a tour of our dreary quarters, and then they led us through the gates of the orphanage and into the bright warmth of the New York sunshine. We chatted in German as we walked down tree-lined streets to a nearby park. The four of us settled snugly on a wrought-iron bench and watched the birds at play in the surrounding trees. Simon drew a verbal picture of life in Pueblo.

"You are going to love it in Pueblo," Simon said. "There will be lots of things for you to do."

"How will we get there?" I asked impatiently. "And when do we go?"

"You will leave in a few days, after all the papers are completed," Simon said. "First, you will take a plane to Colorado, and Opa, your grandfather, will meet you in Denver where your plane lands. Then you'll take a nice train ride to Pueblo."

Uncle Simon and Aunt Esther in New York City in 1950. They came to visit Suzanne and Eric, who had just arrived in America.

"How will I know Opa?" I asked.

"He will be looking for you, but let me describe him. He is a short man with gray hair, and he will be dressed in a business suit. I will call and tell him what you and Suzanne look like, so it will be easy," Simon reassured me.

We walked back to the orphanage as a family, and the warmth of the May sun and Simon's kindness melted some of my fears.

"These relatives here are nice people. Life in America will be good," I promised myself.

The feeling of well-being was reinforced as Simon gave me a parting gift. My blue eyes widened with joy as I peered into the brightly decorated bag he presented. I felt dizzy as I inhaled the sweet smell of chocolates mixed with the tart odor of lemon drops. I had never seen such a treasure chest; there were at least fifty pieces of wrapped candy, and they were all for me!

My sweet tooth took over. I grabbed a chocolate out of the bag and impatiently peeled back the silver wrapping as soon as Simon and Esther walked out the door. Popping the chocolate in my mouth, I caressed it with my tongue and let the sweet sensation overtake my senses. The chocolate melted all too soon, and I couldn't bear to lose the sweetness that filled my mouth. I grabbed another chocolate to preserve the taste. I couldn't stop. I ate another piece, then gobbled another. Finally I forced myself to stash the paper bag of riches under my clothing in the little dormitory dresser.

I was like a lover savoring the sweetness of a first kiss. I couldn't resist going back for more. All through that evening and the following morning, I kept sneaking back to my dresser drawer for just one more sweet. The candy sack was empty, and my stomach was bloated by the next afternoon. Suddenly I was overcome by a wave of nausea. I raced down the hall to the communal bathroom, barely arriving in time at the long row of toilets. I knelt on the cold, white tile floor and learned the lesson of overindulgence.

A caretaker heard the rumbles of my quaking tummy, and she rushed into the bathroom. She helped me clean up, then pried and prodded until I confessed my sins of indulgence. Unbeknownst to me, she warned Simon and Esther to leave the gift of candy behind on their next visit.

Simon never mentioned the incident to me, and I quickly forgot it. Later, in Pueblo, however, Oma would regularly remind me what happened when I was given too much freedom, and the candy incident would become part of my history.

Simon and Esther visited again to give us the news that we would be leaving for Pueblo the next day. Simon had to work, and they could not accompany us to the airport, so once again a social worker was our companion. We got into a car and headed for LaGuardia with our well-worn suitcases in tow.

The plane trip was long and tiresome, and I was eager to arrive in Denver. The big western sky was filled with the glowing colors of sunset as our plane made its descent into Denver. We rushed anxiously into Stapleton Airport's terminal building. I glanced up at the clock. It was 6:25, confirming my stomach's conviction that it was dinnertime.

We filed past the waiting crowd, and a short old man, his face deeply creased by the hardships of a lifetime, came forward. All traces of youthful softness had been erased by years of Nazi persecution. He introduced himself in German as Opa, our grandfather.

"How old and hard this man looks," I thought with surprise. I didn't know what I had expected, but I knew I hadn't anticipated anyone quite this old.

There was no time for idle chatter. Our plane had arrived late, and we had not a minute to spare. Opa hustled us quickly to baggage claim, and we hurriedly grabbed our cardboard suitcases off the conveyor belt, then rushed outside to catch a taxi to Union Station, about fifteen minutes away.

Opa had been in America for eleven years, and his English was good. He managed to relay his sense of urgency to the cab driver, and we were whisked to the train station just in time to board.

By this time I was starving, but I was afraid to say a word. I realized that we had no time to stop, and I didn't want to make a bad first impression. Instead, I found a water fountain and took a quick drink.

The train was very dark, and the ride seemed to take forever. We chatted in German to Opa about New York and

Eric and Uncle Willie in the dirt street in front of the Pueblo bungalow where Eric spent his first years in America.

Pueblo. He tried to set our minds at ease by describing our new home. His kind manner belied the hardness of his face.

"What do you do in Pueblo?" I asked. He tried to explain his work as a junk man, traversing the back alleys of Pueblo, seeking items that he could recycle. He promised that I could come along in his truck sometime.

Opa told us that his son Willie, who worked the 3:00 to 11:00 p.m. shift as a hotel bellboy, would meet us at the Pueblo station with the truck.

The train chugged to a stop in Pueblo after the tiresome three-hour journey. We walked outside into the dark, cool night, and Willie, a handsome blonde in his twenties, met us with a wide grin. Opa acted as translator as the four of us squeezed into the old black pickup truck.

We pulled to a stop in front of a small bungalow located on a dirt street. The lights in the house were ablaze as the tires crunched to a stop in the yard. Oma and Elsie, our seventeen-year-old aunt, awaited our arrival. The front door opened into a small living room. We entered the low-ceilinged room, and I was struck by the cramped conditions.

Where our two-story house in Leutesdorf had been made of stone, with high ceilings and a huge, formal living room, this was a one-story wooden bungalow. The small living room opened on to an even smaller kitchen on one side and a bedroom on the other. Behind the first bedroom was a second, tiny bedroom. I wondered where the six of us would sleep.

I soon learned that the kitchen would be my bedroom. A cot had been placed on the wall under the kitchen window next to the table. It was there, in the middle of the household, with not a modicum of privacy, I would spend my early teen-age years.

Oma and Opa sat in the front yard of their tiny Pueblo home.

Everybody was exhausted, and after a few words of greeting, we all headed to bed. I quickly settled down in my kitchen cot and fell fast asleep. I slept soundly and didn't hear Opa and Willie leave for work or Elsie leave for school the next morning. Finally, sunlight streamed in the east-facing window and woke me for the first day of my new life in Colorado.

Chapter Six

"You'll Never Amount to Anything"

It was already May when we arrived in Pueblo, and Oma immediately enrolled us in Fountain Elementary School so that we could begin to learn English. The school was only a mile down the road, a straight walk, and Suzanne and I made our own way after the first day.

We were placed in a special class to learn English. American children, curious about the newcomers, ran up to us in the playground.

"How are you?" they asked, waiting to hear our thickly accented response.

"Okay," I quickly learned to answer. "How are you?"

At first, their quick reply was gibberish, but I soon learned to communicate in playground English.

At home, Oma and Opa spoke to us in English as much as possible, easing the transition to a new tongue. Elsie and Willie, having left Germany as young children, knew no German, and we communicated through hand gestures and through Oma and Opa.

School was out for the summer a few weeks after we arrived in Pueblo, and we were on vacation. I was unaccustomed to summers off, and at first I was at loose ends. But Oma and Opa soon put me to work. Opa taught me about his junk business little by little. When he returned from a day of collecting odds and ends, I helped him unload the truck.

First, I learned to stack the rags in the big shed at the back of the yard. Then Opa taught me how to sort the metals, separating the more valuable brass and copper from the iron. To the passer-by, our backyard looked like a garden overrun with weeds of junk, but Opa had a special place for each item.

Brass bedposts were valuable collectibles, and my job was to strip the brass from the iron beneath. I used a hammer and chisel to cautiously peel back the layer of brass, attempting to save as much of the precious metal as possible. With the delicate touch of a surgeon, I finished the tedious job with pliers and placed the two metals in separate piles. Then I picked up another post. The work never ran out because as much as I accomplished during the day, Opa's foray into the alleys of Pueblo brought another mound of work.

The yard was warm and dusty, and I sought shade under the few small trees. My hands sweated inside my cloth gloves, and the sun braised my shoulders as it crept across the summer sky, defining my working hours. I had no chance to practice English alone in the yard, and chisel against metal was the only sound I heard.

I occasionally escaped from the tedium of the yard when Willie couldn't ride in the truck with Opa. Then Opa invited me to serve as helper and taste the freedom of the open road. We criss-crossed the alleys of Pueblo, and I waved my right arm out the window, ringing a brass bell.

"Stop, I have something for you," the housewives hollered out their back windows. Then they rushed to us with their precious junk, armed for barter.

Opa, a good-humored man, chatted glibly in English with the housewives as he purchased their rags, metals, glass, cast-iron stoves and mattresses. Sometimes, the items were so heavy, Opa and I both had to lift them into the truck. I picked up some more English as well as business acumen as I watched him work.

Opa was generally mild-mannered, but he couldn't bear greedy clients. If a woman demanded too much money for some metal, Opa turned red with anger.

"Forget it," Opa shouted. He slammed the truck door with finality and launched down the alley.

Opa was always kind to me. He knew my weakness for sweets and indulged me. Mom-and-pop grocery stores dotted our route, and Opa stopped and bought us each a Nehi orange soda. I savored the feeling of the cold, wet bottle in my sweaty hands and the sweet taste in my dry mouth.

When we got hungry, Opa parked at the wide end of the alley and unwrapped the sandwiches that Oma had packed. We chatted in English. I was filled with a sense of well-being and happiness at our special time together.

Visits from aunts and uncles broke the monotony of the daily routine. Aunt Molly arrived with her husband from California, and Eddie, who had left home only a short time earlier, came to see us. Their visits were an excuse for vacation, and we took day trips to the dramatic Royal Gorge, the 1,000-foot canyon carved by the Arkansas River. It was only an hour's trip from Pueblo, and I looked forward to staring down the mouth of the seemingly bottomless chasm.

During one visit from Aunt Molly, an incident occurred that changed my status in the family. Molly, Oma and I went to the Crews-Beggs store to buy me some new clothes.

I entered the store, and my mouth fell open in awe. Never had I seen anything to match this magnificence. Rows of clothing lined the walls, and shelves of treasures lined the aisles like an endless string of jewels. We took the escalator up to the second floor, and I gaped speechlessly. Efficient as a seasoned bargain-hunter, Oma quickly found some inexpensive slacks and shirts from the treasure trove of choices.

"It's time to go, Erich," Oma said as I wandered in wonder through the racks of clothing.

My eye caught sight of a baseball glove and ball as we descended on the escalator. I picked them up and placed the glove on my hand, relishing the feeling of the supple leather against my fingers as they firmly gripped the ball. I lagged behind as Oma approached the cashier. I was still wearing the mitt and clasping the ball. She laid my clothing on the counter and got ready to pay.

"What about the glove and ball?" the clerk asked as she finished ringing up the merchandise. Oma turned around and looked at me with surprise. Red crept up her neck as she flushed with embarrassment. Then fury supplanted shame, and the red flamed across her face.

"Erich, put that down," Oma seethed. "You are a bad boy, trying to steal!"

With my primitive English skills, I couldn't figure out what the clerk had said to make Oma so angry. I looked at Oma with a mixture of bewilderment and despair. I had not planned to steal,

I simply wanted to hold the glove. I was totally confused by the furor. I cringed as I skulked over to the shelf to return the glove. Rather than defend myself, I withdrew into a protective shell.

We walked home in uneasy silence. Only the quick tapping of Oma's shoes along the pavement revealed her anger. Finally, Oma spoke.

"You are a bad boy, not to be trusted. In New York, you ate all the candy. Today, you tried to steal. You are as worthless as your Vater," Oma taunted. "You'll never amount to anything."

Labeled a thief, I had nothing left to lose. So I lived up to my reputation, and one more incident sealed my fate as a sinner. Each Friday morning, Oma sent me to the bakery downtown to buy the challah, the Sabbath bread. It was a long walk, about two miles, and I was expected to go straight to the bakery and back.

I noticed a candy store on my route, and my sweet tooth craved a simple treat. But Oma gave me only the exact change needed to buy the challah, and I had no money of my own to satisfy my burning desire for sweets.

"Why not ask people on the streets for some change? Oma will never know, and I can buy some sweets," I mused.

I approached passers-by with the doleful eyes of an orphan. "Please do you have a few cents for me?" I begged in my sweet, heavily accented voice.

I had easy success. I only had to approach a few people before I pocketed enough change to visit the candy store on the way home.

I had my first treat when I got to the bakery. The bakery always had a tray of doughnut samples on the counter, and I started my morning indulgence by filling my mouth with the samples.

I bought the challah, then headed up the street to the candy store. I painstakingly perused the vast choice of treasures

Opa, Oma, Aunt Elsie and Eric posed for the camera in Pueblo, 1955.

and finally settled on a package of Kits. I walked slowly home, savoring the chewy, caramel flavor and my success as a beggar.

One day on my way to the bakery, I made the fatal mistake of begging from a woman who was Oma's friend. She recognized me and immediately spilled the story to Oma. My trips to the bakery were brought to a quick halt.

I was condemned to the yard for the rest of the summer. When the family took day trips, I stayed behind peeling the aluminum layer off basketsful of metal spheres that came from bedposts. As endless as the summer days, the baskets lined the yard, covering every square inch of available space. Day after day I faced those spheres; no longer was the tedium broken by the highly anticipated forays in the truck; no longer did I go out for challah. I had lost all rights to leave the house.

My favorite part of the week was Sunday night when I could lay in bed and listen to the Hit Parade on the radio. But first, Oma and Opa listened to the news with Walter Winchell. I always looked forward to hearing his voice and his opening words, "Good evening Mr. and Mrs. North and South America and all the ships at sea. Let's go to press."

One Sunday Winchell had serious news, and the Hit Parade was pre-empted by President Harry Truman. He announced that we had declared war on Korea. I had no idea where Korea was, but Oma was overwhelmed with anxiety. She feared that her favorite son, Willie, would be sent off to war. And indeed, Willie was drafted that summer and sent to Fort Leonard, Missouri. Oma was sick with worry until Willie was assigned to Japan instead of Korea.

Another pleasure from my bed under the kitchen window was spying on my libidinous neighbor. I eagerly awaited the crunch of the 1949 Chevy's tires on the dirt road, which meant the eighteen-year-old teen who lived across the street had arrived home with her beau. I got up on my elbow to get a clear view of the ardent couple parked across the narrow road. They quickly got into some heavy necking, and my budding sexual urges were vicariously gratified.

I dreaded Mondays as much as I loved Sunday nights. Most days, I looked forward to lunch because it provided a break from the routine of my work in the yard. But Monday was lentil soup day. When Oma called me in on Mondays, I approached the kitchen with dread. A lump grew in my throat as I entered the back door and faced the generous bowlful of grayish brown glop. Without a word, I sat down at the table with Oma and Suzanne and slowly spooned the loathsome stuff down my throat, taking frequent drinks of water to drown the awful taste. Finally, the bottom of the bowl was in sight, and I was safe for another week.

I didn't even consider telling Oma how much I hated that soup. She was from the old school, and you finished whatever was placed before you with gratitude. And I didn't want to give her another excuse to mock me.

Oma watched me like a cat ready to pounce at any sign of weakness ever since the Crews-Beggs incident. I was forever labeled as a bad boy, and I cowered under her bitter taunts.

When Oma laughed at me, she made me feel two inches tall. Sometimes, she tried to get Suzanne as an ally, cajoling Suzanne to laugh along at the hapless Erich who would never amount to anything. Oma resorted to German, spitting words of mockery and reminding me of Vater, who had abandoned me.

With Oma's insults and the unrelenting, unrewarding work of the yard, I had little to make me proud that summer. The disapproving looks from Vater's icy blue eyes had been replaced by Oma's. My feelings of self-worth sank to new depths as Vater's buried criticisms resurfaced under Oma's reminders.

When September finally came, I enrolled in Risley Junior High. By then my English was good enough to get along, and I was placed in regular classes. I walked home each day for lunch, so lentil soup remained a steady part of my diet.

I was still expected to work in the yard after school. As winter approached, I was assigned the chore of chopping wood for the family wood stove. The wood was piled in a shed in the far corner of the backyard, and I spent hours in the cold shed wielding an ax. Finally, Oma called me in for dinner. I spent the hours until bedtime doing my homework.

Opa stopped work early on Friday nights, and I was allowed to quit my wood chopping when he got home. We all took baths, dressed in our finest clothing and sat down together to welcome the Sabbath. Opa made a ritual of saying the prayers over the Manischewitz wine and challah. After our traditional chicken dinner, we walked together to the shul, the United Hebrew Center.

The United Hebrew Center in Pueblo, the synagogue where Eric learned Hebrew and had his bar mitzvah.

We went back to the temple for Saturday morning services. All the Jewish families of Pueblo dressed in their Sabbath best, and it was clear that our family was very poor in comparison. Saturday was a good day because I was freed from work in the yard. Sometimes, Elsie, who was a senior in high school, took us on the bus to the movies. We learned about the Wild West and what it was like to be a real American by watching Gene Autry and Roy Rogers.

Soon after my arrival in Pueblo, Opa started tutoring me in Hebrew and the Torah in preparation for my bar mitzvah. Opa was patient yet firm as he insisted that I perform the entire service in Hebrew, and we spent long evenings together studying the language. It was one more chore to endure.

I faced the day of my bar mitzvah, in March 1951, with dread, unsure of my skill in Hebrew. But I performed well, and I was very pleased with myself. The Women's Auxiliary of the United Hebrew Center presented me with a Bible, and there was cake and coffee for the members of the congregation.

Vater didn't write very often, but I always looked forward to getting mail from him. When the letters came, I would pore over his German descriptions of the business and life with Theresa, who had stayed on as his housekeeper. I would write back immediately, telling him how well I was doing in school and about my election to the National Honor Society.

Approximately eighteen months after we came to America, Vater wrote that he was getting married. He also sent a document for us to sign because the Germans were paying war reparations to survivors. We sent the document back, and the letters from Vater abruptly halted. Day after day, I approached the mailbox with expectation, but nothing ever came. I finally stopped anticipating mail after months without a word.

I convinced Oma and Opa to let me get a job during my eighth grade year. I started by doing some yard work for Bud Garon, who my grandparents knew through the synagogue. After I spent a few afternoons at his house, Bud invited me to work at his shop, Western States Novelty on Union Avenue in downtown Pueblo. The small, narrow store was crammed with odds and ends, from party favors to squirt guns to costume jewelry. Calendars with pinup pictures were hidden under the counter for sale to those who asked.

I went to Bud's store straight from school by bus and stayed until closing at six. Bud had an old Chevy carryall that he used for sales trips around the state, and he often gave me a ride home after work.

I did odd jobs, sweeping the floor and straightening the shelves. An easy-going man with a big heart, Bud was patient and kind with me. Working for him gave me freedom from

Oma's watchful eyes, some pocket money and a sense of self-worth. Unlike Oma, Bud never once criticized nor mocked me. Once I got to know the ropes, he often went off to visit his friend Sam in the furniture store next door, leaving me to run the novelty shop.

One day, Bud went next door, and a man came in for pinup pictures. I leaned under the counter and pulled out the cellophane-wrapped packets. I felt the heat of

Bud Garon, Eric's first boss, lounged in the doorway of his Western States Novelty Shop in Pueblo in 1953.

embarrassment creeping up my neck as I handed him the contraband. He quickly perused the packets, chose a set and paid me a dollar. I couldn't look him in the eye as I took the money and placed the remaining packets safely back under the counter.

Another time Bud left me alone in the store, and a well-dressed woman came in. She studied the jewelry in the locked glass case and asked to see a rhinestone necklace. I unlocked the case, and with shaky hands, carefully presented her with the glit-

Forty years later, Eric returned to the Pueblo bungalow to remember his teen years there. The bungalow is much the same as it was in the 1950s.

tery strands of faux diamonds. Without even trying it on, she said, "I want this necklace."

She pulled out a wallet stuffed with cash. My eyes nearly popped from their sockets as she handed me the bills.

"Twenty, forty, sixty, eighty, one hundred; twenty and five," she counted as she placed the bills into my sweaty palm. It was 1951, and I had never seen so much cash in my life. I couldn't wait for Bud to get back so I could tell him about my incredible sale.

Bud's one vice was betting on baseball games, and he regularly lost his shirt. When I came to work in the afternoons, Bud was glued to the radio as Red Barber announced the games. The inevitable happened, and his team started to lose. Bud turned red with anger and frustration. But he never took that anger out on me.

Oma and Opa took six of the seven dollars I got paid each week to buy me clothes and other necessities. I spent my dollar on sweets and other treats.

My days were loaded with school, my job, homework, Hebrew lessons and the work I was still expected to do in the backyard, so there was little time for friends. But the Berg family at our synagogue took a liking to me, and they invited me to spend the weekend. Oma and Opa agreed, much to my surprise.

Their family life was charming to me, and I felt so good to be in a loving home. The Bergs were a middle-class family that ate well. Their life was all I had dreamed a home life should be. Love displaced mockery, and the family showed a true enjoyment of being together. I couldn't stand to leave when they told me it was time to go back to Oma's.

"Please let me stay here. I don't want to go back," I pleaded. I spilled my guts about how terrible life was at home and begged them to adopt me.

The Bergs were very sympathetic, but told me it wasn't possible. They drove me back home, and I cringed both with my fear of returning home and my embarrassment at reaching out for the first time in my life.

Oma and Opa never mentioned the incident, but it was clear that the Bergs had told them what happened. I was never invited to the Berg home again although they were always cordial at synagogue.

I didn't know it at the time, but my escape from life with Oma and Opa was imminent. Elsie had graduated from high school and moved to New York, and Oma and Opa were eager to retire and join her there. Their plans did not include my sister and me.

Chapter Seven

"DP Teen-agers Need Foster Home"

Like Vater before them, gradually Oma and Opa made us aware that we were going to be sent away. We were to be placed in foster homes in Denver while our grandparents moved to New York. Oma, Opa and their children must have had long discussions to reach this conclusion, but we were kept in the dark.

We never knew why Oma and Opa decided to retire at that time or why they didn't want to take us along. We never heard any reasons why Simon or Molly, the married children, didn't offer to take us in. The family was shedding its responsibility for us as easily as it had accepted that obligation only three years earlier. Like the useless scraps of metal in Opa's yard, we were to be discarded to lighten their load as they departed for a new life.

I was buffeted by the winds of contrary feelings. I was eager to escape Oma's mockery, but I also feared the unknown. Once again I was being forced into a new home with new rules and a new set of family relationships. But my wellspring of eternal hope bubbled up. From an unknown source of deep faith, I believed that tomorrow would be better, and I was more pleased than worried about leaving Pueblo.

The arrangements began during my ninth-grade year at Centennial High School. Oma and Opa sent Suzanne and me up to Denver on the Continental Trailways bus each month to meet with the social worker who would place us in a new home. The trip provided not only a holiday from school, but also a release from the prison of my backyard duties. The 112-mile bus trip, where I could see the changing seasons reflected on the trees along the highway, afforded me the first taste of a vacation.

A social worker from Jewish Family Service met us at the Denver bus station. She scribbled notes as she asked us about our life in Pueblo and our early history. She developed a thick file on our lives and an empathy for our plight after months of interviews.

Finally, on May 14, 1953, our social worker placed an article in the *Intermountain Jewish News* seeking a home for us. On a page with ads for "The Rado Pad," which was a 1950s arthritis remedy, and the Emerald Room of the Brown Palace Hotel, the newspaper sang our praises, changing our names in a thinly veiled attempt at anonymity.

"DP Teen-agers Need Foster Homes" the headline on top of page eleven shouted. The article stated, "German-born Clara, 13, and Eli, 15, came to the United States three years ago to live with their grandparents. Their mother was a victim of Hitlerism and their dad, still alive in Europe, is unable to care for them. Their grandparents, suffering bad health and financial adversities, are unable to continue raising them to full maturity.

"Clara and Eli are healthy, serious-minded, attractive, industrious, intelligent teen-agers. Honor students in school, with proper opportunities they show signs of being college scholarship material and good citizens of which any community could be proud."

The article goes on to describe me: "Good looking, clean-cut Eli is somewhat shy and reserved. He is eager to make something of himself. After school he can be found working part-time as a salesman in a little shop. That winning smile of his is going to captivate the hearts of young ladies as it already has that of his social worker. The crew cut gives him that 'collegiate' look. His peaches and cream complexion could set any girl green with envy, but it shouldn't be too long before the fuzz appears. (Next on his clothing purchase list simply must be a sweater whose sleeves are long enough for his arms!)"

As slick as a used car ad, the newspaper story brought results. It caught the attention of Bea and Ben Perlmutter, a middle-class Jewish family from west Denver who had a spare bedroom because their daughter had just gotten married. They thought I would be the perfect companion for their seven-year-old son, Joey, but they could not take my sister. That meant that once again, Suzanne and I were to be separated.

Meanwhile, life in Pueblo continued as before. I awoke each morning in my bed under the kitchen window, dressed quickly for school, and headed off to Centennial High. I was a good student, and Oma and Opa had no criticism of me on that account. School provided an escape from Oma's watchful eyes, and while I had few friends, it was a place I felt successful.

After completing ninth grade at Centennial, I spent the summer incarcerated in the yard as the wheels of bureaucracy rolled slowly but inevitably toward our relocation. Then in September 1953, shortly after I started tenth grade, it was time to move to Denver. Suzanne and I packed up our belongings and headed north on the Trailways bus. When we got to Denver, we parted ways, bound for separate, new lives.

I settled in the social worker's car. I was filled with a mixture of anxiety and anticipation. The short ride to west Denver was quiet as I contemplated my new living arrangements. We drove up to a typical 1950s blond brick, ranch-style home on a quiet suburban street.

"These people must be rich," I thought, mentally contrasting my new home to our tiny bungalow on a dirt street in Pueblo. I was awed by the majesty of the large home in a neighborhood of perfectly manicured lawns. The new Buick parked in front of the house cemented my impression of prosperity.

As we entered the house, I was dazzled by the spacious rooms. I was escorted to my own bedroom, an incredible luxury after three years under the kitchen window in Pueblo.

I settled into my room and began to unpack the two shabby suitcases I had brought from Pueblo. Mrs. Perlmutter watched as I carefully placed my ragged sweaters and torn underwear in the dresser drawers.

"Let's go shopping for some new clothes," Mrs. Perlmutter said.

We headed downtown and replaced my well-worn wardrobe with brand-new clothes. Unlike Oma, Mrs. Perlmutter didn't buy only from the clearance racks. Again I felt a sense of economic well-being.

Mrs. Perlmutter immediately enrolled me in North High. Neighbor kids taught me how to hitchhike, and I often got a ride to school so I didn't have to take the bus. I got a job as a caddy at Miller's Grocery store after school to make some spending money.

With the appetite of a deprived teen-ager, I enjoyed the rich, delicious, kosher food Mrs. Perlmutter prepared. My days soon filled with school, work and babysitting for Joey. He and I tossed around a softball in the small backyard when Mrs. Perlmutter went off to play Mah Jongg with her friends.

The Perlmutters tried to make me a part of the family, and each Saturday I attended synagogue with them. After services, Mr. Perlmutter took me on a tour of his construction projects around the city. I was a shy, somber teen-ager without much to say on these trips. Mr. Perlmutter tried to draw me out, but I was afraid to vent my feelings, lest I explode. The sorrow of a life's worth of loneliness stayed bottled up inside.

I had been properly raised by a series of autocrats who had taught me to be seen and not heard. I had occasionally tested their authority with dire consequences, so I acquired the facade of obedience in Vater's house and Oma's. But now I was growing up, and my battles with authority became more frequent. I demonstrated the typical teen's blemishes of rebellion.

"Put on your hat, it's cold outside," Mr. Perlmutter insisted as I headed out the door to hitchhike to school.

He turned back toward the kitchen, and I tossed the cap behind the couch and darted out the door.

I had begun to make some friends at school and wanted to ensure my place in the crowd by having a party. One Saturday, I thought the Perlmutters were going out, and I could surreptitiously invite the gang over.

I snuck over to the phone and hastily called a bunch of friends. Mrs. Perlmutter overheard and rushed into the room.

"What are you doing, Eric? You haven't asked our permission for a party. We're having friends over tonight and need the rec room. You'll have to call your friends back and cancel," she said.

I said nothing, but seethed inside with anger. A typically self-centered teen, I couldn't understand why I couldn't just invite a few friends to the house. After all, I watched Joey all the time, didn't I? Life seemed very unfair.

I was drowning in a whirlpool of emotions. The raging tide of my fifteen-year-old hormones brought waves of anger and rebellion, and cascades of dark depression. A lucky teen-ager finds an adult anchor to steady him through the tempestuous ride of adolescence. I had no one. I had learned at an early age that it was risky to depend on any other human being. My young life had been burdened with too many losses to seek safe harbor in any adult's arms.

The only adult women I could remember had been cruel — first Theresa, then Oma. And the men had abandoned me — first Vater, then Opa. How could I confide in either Mr. or Mrs. Perlmutter? I had no experience with trust.

I went through my months at the Perlmutters in solemn solitude. I felt like a permanent guest in their home rather than a foster son. As I entered the blond brick house after school each day, I was choked by the need to try to fit in. Home was not a place of security, but an ordeal of botched connections.

Even my relationship with Joey was strained. He became another load on my shoulders rather than a playmate and friend. When I came home from school, Mrs. Perlmutter headed off to her Mah Jongg game, and I was stuck babysitting. Once again I was imprisoned by backyard duties. This time it was a young boy rather than brass beds that held me captive.

I continued to meet regularly with my social worker, and I didn't hide my unhappiness with life at the Perlmutters. I saw them as strangers with whom I had nothing in common. They saw me as an ungrateful, rebellious teen-ager.

We surrendered to my history after nine months of trying to become a family. It was not to be. The Perlmutters, my social worker and I decided mutually that I would be better off some-where else.

My social worker had told me about the Jewish National Home for Asthmatic Children, a residential treatment center for asthmatic kids, which also served as a home for a few orphans. I was eager to escape the bondage of a family setting after failures with Vater, Oma and Opa, and the Perlmutters. I jumped at the chance to live in a place where there would be lots of people my own age.

I packed up my hopes and my suitcases, this time filled with trendy new clothes, and we piled in the family Buick on June 13, 1954, and drove to the Children's Home.

Although the Home was only a few short blocks from the Perlmutters' brick ranch, I felt I was traveling to a new world. A sense of relief washed over me as I bid the Perlmutters goodbye. I arrived at the Home full of hope, and from the very start, it truly felt like home.

I was greeted by Joe Flood, the young, happy-go-lucky house-parent in the teen dormitory. Flood showed me to a small, com-fortable room in the new Simon building, a long, one-story, brick dormitory housing twenty-four teen girls on one side and twenty-four boys on the other. The two wings were separated by a door that was locked at night. My cheery room overlooking the Home's grounds had bunk beds for two, a closet, dresser and built-in desk. Each side of the building had a communal bathroom.

The Home covered several square blocks in west Denver near 19th Avenue and Julian Street, a residential neighborhood of brick bungalows. In addition to the dorms, there was a hospi-tal for the asthmatic children. The grounds included a baseball field, playground and basketball court. The large dining hall served kosher food to the hundred young residents between the ages of six and eighteen.

The remedy for childhood asthma in the 1950s was to separate children from their parents and treat their asthma both medically and emotionally. Kids stayed at the home from eighteen to twenty-four months, and the parents couldn't visit for the first six months. Most of the residents came from the East Coast.

The Home was started in 1907 by Fannie Lorber, who organized auxiliaries of Jewish women around the country to provide financial support. Each year, the auxiliary presidents and delegates were invited to visit the Home for a conference. We'd put on a real show, polishing all the wood and chrome, manicuring the gardens and making everything look homey. One evening during the convention, we acted out skits for the distinguished guests.

My first friend at the home was Joel Cohen. On Sunday, my second day there, Joel invited me to join a group of teens who were going to sneak off the hospital grounds, ride the bus to City Park lake and go boating. After lunch, we went back to the Simon Building and concocted our scheme. We met some girls from the other side of the building and casually strolled across the grounds and off the property.

Unfortunately, to reach the street, we had to walk by the quarters of Jack Gershtenson, the Home's administrator, called "Mr. G." by the residents. Mr. G. ran the Home like a tight ship, and when he saw us passing by, he immediately called the houseparent, Joe Flood, to inquire about our exploits.

Flood was waiting for us when we returned from our illicit excursion. He had some bad news. We were to report to Mr. G.'s office first thing Monday morning. We were guilty on two counts: leaving the grounds without permission and boating on the lake.

It was only my second day there, and I was already in hot water. I slept restlessly that night, not knowing what to expect from Mr. G., whom I had never met. Would the punishment be meted out in Oma's way, and would I once again be the subject of ridicule?

I quivered with fear as I marched with my six fellow criminals down the long hall of the administration building to Mr. G.'s office. As I followed the others into the office, I got a glimpse of a stout, fifty-year-old man chomping hard on a fat cigar. Mr. G., dressed in suit and tie, remained seated behind his desk as he looked us over.

"I'm sure you know why you're here," Mr. G. stated in a tone that banned dissent.

We nodded our heads in affirmation.

"You all know the rules at the Home?" our guardian asked rhetorically.

"Yes," we said in unison.

"You are confined to grounds for two weeks and may leave only to go to work," Mr. G. said.

"Yes, sir," we agreed sheepishly.

We turned to leave his office, and my shoulders sagged in relief. The punishment was fair and just, and I could easily live with it. There was no ridicule, no long-lasting effects, and I had made some new friends. "This Home is truly a better tomorrow," I thought.

I would have many occasions to experience Mr. G.'s brand of justice through the years. A father figure to all the kids, he treated everyone equally, never getting too close to any single child. His sense of fair play meant he rarely bent or broke a rule for anyone.

When I got to the Home, I was already sixteen, and the friends I made at school were starting to drive. No one who lived at the Home had ever earned permission to drive, but with my stubborn will, I was determined to be the first.

I lived at the Home for a few months before I mustered the courage to approach Mr. G. I stopped to see Bert Mock, Mr. G.'s long-time secretary, and requested an appointment with the chief.

"What do you want to talk to Mr. Gershtenson about?" Bert asked.

"I want to get a driver's permit," I told her.

She raised her eyebrows in surprise but silently made an appointment for the next day.

I arrived at my appointment armed with an arsenal of rationale. Mr. G. chomped on his cigar as he pondered my request. His yellow, protruding teeth barely freed the cigar as he responded.

"This is against the rules. No one who lives here is permitted to drive," the boss reminded me.

I persisted, reminding him that my situation was different.

"I'm not like the others. I'll be here until I graduate from high school. I have no other home to return to. It's not fair that I can't drive," I pleaded.

"I'll think about it," Mr. G. finally said.

I was back at Bert's desk two weeks later, requesting another appointment, then a third. With my stubborn perseverance, I was trying to wear down the firm, fair leader of the Home. Finally Mr. G. said he had to check with the Board of Directors. I got the good news two weeks later.

"The Board has agreed to make an exception in your case. You can get a driver's permit as long as you keep your school grades up," Mr. G. decreed.

I couldn't wait to start driving. I asked Nate Davidovich, whose father was the rabbi at the Home, to teach me. Nate had become a good friend, and I walked to his home often, hoping that his mother had a fresh batch of her wonderful chocolate chip cookies waiting. I was rewarded not only with a mouthful of heaven, but also with a saintly friend.

Nate had the patience of Job and took me out for a driving lesson in his old black jalopy each Sunday. The car had a standard transmission, and I jerked it around an empty parking lot. I thought I would never learn as our ears were assaulted by the cacophony of grinding gears.

Nate decreed after several weeks that I was ready for a test run around Sloan's Lake. The beautiful west Denver lake, just a few blocks from the Home, provided ample opportunity for practice. The area around it included some upscale residential streets, but also Sheridan Boulevard, busy with shops and the local drive-in theatre. It was a true test of my skill.

Nate's confidence in me and my undying patience brought me the self-assurance I needed to succeed. I made it around the lake without incident. Nate and I felt flushed with the success of teacher and student who had mastered a difficult skill.

I was ready for the driving test after a few more weeks of practice. Nate lent me his car, and I passed the test on the first try. Having a driver's license was a milestone. It meant that I was an all-American teen-age boy!

The thrill of having a license soon wore thin. What good was a license if I had nothing to drive? It was inevitable that I soon would get itchy to buy a car.

I was working every day after school, and I was able to put about $300 in the bank by the summer of 1955. I was determined to spend my free time that summer behind the wheel of my very own car. I could picture myself driving my friends around Sloan's Lake or up Federal Boulevard to the A&W Root Beer Stand. I wanted a car so badly, I could smell the leather of the plush seats.

There was only one little obstacle. I would have to beg again for Mr. G.'s permission. The task seemed even more formidable, but so was my will. I knew I had an airtight reason: I had gotten a new job at Colorado Engraving in downtown Denver, and it was too far to walk. So once again I went to Bert Mock to make an appointment with the chief.

I entered Mr. G.'s office confident he would see my need.

"Mr. G., I've kept up my grades, and I'm a responsible resident of the Home. I have a new job downtown, and I really need a car to get there," I said.

He gnawed on his cigar, leaned over his desk and stared into my eyes. "Eric, there are buses that can take you downtown. You don't need a car to get to that job."

"My hours are irregular, and a car would be much more convenient. I promise I'll be responsible," I vowed.

Mr. G. continued gazing at me in silence. Finally he said he would think it over. Again we had to have several meetings before he finally relented. But surrender he did, and I couldn't wait to buy my car.

Nate, my driving teacher, took me shopping for a car. I became the proud owner of a 1949 brown Ford. Having my own set of wheels filled me with joy. I had struggled all my life for a sense of freedom, and with this car, I had it. Behind the wheel of my Ford, I could take control of my destiny. I steered around the streets of Denver to my job at Colorado Engraving with an unparalleled feeling of power. My Ford was my passport to the American dream.

It was the happiest time in my young life. The Home provided a sense of security without making the demands of family life. I was doing well in school, and my job provided gas money for the Ford.

I also was starting to have success with girls. One of my partners in crime in the City Park incident was Judy Gilbert, who became my first flame. An asthmatic, Judy stayed at the Home for about six months after I arrived.

I was nervous about asking a girl for a date, so we participated in group activities with other residents of the Home. Our romance budded slowly as brand-new sensations stirred in my adolescent soul. Judy and I spent evenings holding hands as we roller skated around the Mammoth Gardens rink. When we went bowling at Sloan's Lake Bowl, we sat snuggled on the bench, reluctantly separating when it was our turn to roll the ball.

I was deep in the throes of my first crush, and I showered Judy with small gifts. I finally had the courage to ask Judy for a formal date. But it came too late. She was declared well enough to leave the Home. I bought her a gold Jewish star as a going-away present, and we bid each other a tearful farewell.

She left for New York on a cold day in December 1954. I thought I might die. How would I live without my first girl-friend? I had finally awakened to the pleasures of friendship with the opposite sex, and now Judy was gone. I wrote to her almost every day, telling her about the happenings at the Home and how much I was missing her.

But with the fickleness of youth, I soon started looking at the local girls. That's when I met Doris Kaplan, who lived outside the Home. Doris was part of the crowd I met through Joel Cohen, the ringleader of the City Park escapade. I got permission to leave the Home on Friday nights and met our crowd, about a dozen boys and girls. We took turns going to each of their homes. We commandeered their family rooms and spent the evening chatting and dancing to forty-five rpm recordings of Elvis Presley and Nat King Cole.

Doris, a petite brunette with short, curly hair, was a dynamo. Her warm smile lit up the room, and everybody liked her. I was drawn to her energy like a magnet, and we soon became an "item." When we danced together, our bodies became one. Our rhythms matched perfectly.

I was seventeen and on top of the world. I could forget about my past when I was with Doris and live the dream of being a normal American teen-ager, replete with girlfriend and car. Doris had reawakened my belief in a better tomorrow. Wrapped in her embrace, I found the sense of security that had evaded me since infanthood. I had not been hugged since being torn from my mother's arms, and I clung to Doris like a love-starved puppy.

When I finished working as a janitor at Colorado Engraving each Saturday afternoon, I lovingly polished my Ford and daydreamed about my date with Doris. We were going dancing! I took a shower in the dormitory bathroom, shined my white buckskins, combed my hair and smiled at my image in the mirror. Life was good.

At 7:00 p.m. I got in the big brown Ford and steered down the west Denver streets with their large elm trees and small brick homes. Doris' modest white stucco house was in a Jewish neighborhood less than a mile southwest of the Home.

I got out of the Ford and rushed to Doris' door, eager to begin our evening together. Mrs. Kaplan answered the door, and I chatted easily with her and her husband as I waited for Doris to put the finishing touches on her outfit. While I was awkward with most adults, Doris' parents made me feel welcome. Going to Doris' house was like going home.

Finally Doris emerged. She was dressed in her dancing skirt, her bright eyes greeting me with love, and she took my breath away. As I opened the car door for her, my heart nearly burst with happiness.

Our destination was Elitch's, Denver's premier amusement park, which also housed the best dance hall in town — the Trocadero. We drove west along Sloan's Lake to Sheridan Boulevard, site of my first driving test. The first few blocks were filled with shops and the drive-in theatre. As we moved north, we drove into a residential neighborhood of brick bungalows owned by Italian families. I turned east on West 38th Avenue and back into a commercial area of neighborhood shops. We paid little attention to the scenery as we bubbled with conversation, excited about the imminent evening of dancing.

I drove into the Elitch's parking lot at West 38th and Tennyson and went around the car to open Doris' door. We approached the entrance and caught a glimpse of the giant roller coaster, overshadowing all the other rides. We wandered around the grounds, arm-in-arm, passing the haunted house, the merry-go-round and the Ferris wheel. I stopped at a carnival game and tossed some balls at a basket in a futile attempt to win a Teddy bear for Doris.

Elitch's was famous for its finely manicured flower gardens. A riot of color filled the grounds in summertime when the pansies, peonies, daisies, snapdragons and hundreds of other varieties of flowers were in bloom. With cavalier grace, I leaned into the fountain, pulled out a fresh carnation and presented it to Doris with a flourish.

We strolled over to the Trocadero and joined people of all ages who were lined up at the doors of the dance hall. The Tommy Dorsey and Glen Miller bands were among the favorites who performed there in the summer of 1955. The Trocadero had a roof and a wooden dance floor, but the sides were open, providing dancers with a picturesque view of the gardens. The music, the scenery and the security of Doris' arms permeated all the needy places in my soul.

Doris and I had a favorite song, "Mississippi Mud," a fast jitterbug, and we developed a routine to it. When the band began playing the familiar tune, we smiled at each other and danced into action. Awed by our energy, the dancers around us stopped, formed a circle and cheered us on. It was as if we were made to dance together. I wished the dance would never end.

We left the dance hall in an aura of happiness, and I drove the Ford slowly around the Italian and Jewish neighborhoods, trying to prolong our time together. Flushed with the heat of our dancing and youthful passion, I stopped the car on a deserted street corner and turned off the headlights. I pulled Doris toward me, wrapped my arms around her and placed my lips tightly against hers. We groped at each other in the dark car until I made myself stop. Despite the lack of parenting, I was properly trained in the rules of 1950s courtship, and I never allowed myself to go too far with Doris.

Dates with Doris filled the summer of that glorious year, and I started my senior year at North High School filled with love and hope. I looked forward to Friday nights when our crowd attended the football game, then piled into the Ford and headed over to the A&W for a root beer float. Doris and I dated regularly.

Everyone assumed Doris and I would go together when the time came for the Homecoming dance that fall. But for some reason, I dragged my feet and didn't ask her. As the big day approached, my sister told me that her friend, DeAnna, a ravishing girl I had always admired, didn't yet have a date. I was tempted by DeAnna's beauty and called to ask her to Homecoming. I realized I had made a terrible mistake from the moment DeAnna accepted.

What have you done? You've jeopardized your relationship with Doris for this one date with DeAnna, I chided myself.

The news of my betrayal traveled quickly through our crowd, but Doris said nothing. Instead, she accepted a date with Alan Mandel, and I was history. I called Doris after the dance, but it was too late.

"I made a terrible mistake, Doris, and I'm so unhappy without you," I pleaded. "Please give me another chance."

Doris' voice chilled my soul with its icy indifference. "I had a great time with Alan, and I'm going to see him again," Doris said, clearly conveying that my mistake was not to be forgiven. Indeed, Alan and Doris continued to date and married right after high school.

I spent the rest of my senior year nursing a broken heart. Over and over, I blamed myself for losing Doris. My life had been filled with a string of losses, and I had created the most recent one. I constantly relived the events of the weeks before Homecoming, trying in vain to understand what I had done. I wanted desperately to make it end differently. I was obsessed day and night with a fantasy that Doris would come back to me. The thought possessed a corner of my mind and heart for decades.

I confided my sorrow to Mr. G. and my new houseparent, Ray Resnick. Ray understood what it was like to be spurned by a woman. He had been jilted at the altar, and he came to the Home a broken man. He and I spent hours talking, but there was nothing he could do to lessen my pangs of regret.

Finally, I found escape from the ache of losing Doris in long-distance running. I spent winter afternoons racing around Sloan's Lake. At first, when I approached the 17th Avenue side of the lake, I was stung by the vision of Doris at my side as we drove down that street on our way to Elitch's. I ran faster, trying to outrun the memories. Speed became an antidote for pain. With running I could leave my past in the dust and bolt for the future.

When tryouts came for the high school track team in March, I was ready. I wasn't a natural athlete, so I couldn't compete in the short races where speed was of the essence. But my stubborn determination served me well in providing the stamina for long-distance running. The team had one champion long-distance runner, but there was room for another, and coach Ed Getsch accepted me.

With the persistence that was my trademark, I was determined to make the coach proud. I ran with the team after school each day and competed each weekend. I was no champion and never finished in the top three in any of our meets against the other Denver teams. But I kept on practicing, convinced I could do better. It was my senior year and the last chance I would have to run in the citywide meet. I gave it all I had in the preliminary trials and managed to qualify for the end-of-year citywide meet at South High.

Parents, pals and girlfriends from across Denver cheered on their favorite runner in the large South High stadium. I stepped up to the starting line without a fan in sight. Once again I felt totally alone in the world. Not only was I without family, but also I had lost Doris, my first true love. The truth was, as hard as I ran to forget, I still missed her terribly. I would have given anything to have her in the stands watching me run.

I pushed thoughts of loneliness out of mind and got ready to run. My will to succeed energized my legs, and I ran around the track with single-minded determination. I crossed the finish line, amazed to learn that I had managed a fifth-place finish. My feeling of desolation returned. "Oh Doris, if only you were here to share this moment," I thought.

I continued working at Colorado Engraving and to keep my weekends occupied, I also took a job stuffing newspapers at the *Denver Post*. From 8:00 p.m to 4:30 a.m. each Saturday, I stuffed comics and other sections into the Sunday paper. It was good money, and it kept me from thinking about how I'd rather be dancing with Doris.

I was still convalescing from my lost love when graduation came in June 1956. The graduation ceremony was a dismal event, and I couldn't wait for it to end. Most of my friends were paired up, and Doris was there with Alan. Everyone else went out and partied, but I retreated, like a bruised child, to the security of the Home.

I spent the summer of 1956 working, saving money and getting ready to go to college. I had been accepted to the University of Colorado with a scholarship. Although I was eager to start college, I was scared to leave the blanket of security that the Home had provided. The last two-and-a-half years had been the happiest times of my life. Now, once again, I was being forced from the nest to be on my own.

Chapter Eight

Run for My Life

The summer flew by, and before I felt quite ready, it was time to start life as a college man at the University of Colorado at Boulder. I had a half-tuition scholarship, and I looked for a way to keep my costs down.

The dorms were too rich for my blood, so I moved into the basement of the Trumble family home, a few blocks from campus. Mr. Trumble, a major in the Air Force, worked in the ROTC program at CU. He and his wife had two young children, and in exchange for the room, I babysat for the children and did the yard work.

I arrived on the University of Colorado campus alone and was overcome by its size. I was accustomed to the small campus of North High School, and I had never beheld anything as large as this. Even the imposing Flatirons, the foothills to the west of campus, seemed dwarfed by the majesty of the campus.

The stately flagstone buildings, crowned with red tile roofs, engulfed me. The buildings looked more alike than different, and I wondered how I would ever tell them apart. How would I find my classes? Would I make it across the expansive campus lawns in time to get from one class to the next?

I wandered around looking for the registrar, passing freshmen still wrapped in the cocoon of family security as their parents guided them around campus. I felt like a tourist in a foreign land as I tried to find my way. Feelings of loneliness flooded over me, and the sense of being different, which I had worked so hard to suppress, rose up and choked me with fear.

My first semester was crowded with bad decisions. First, I chose to enroll in the architectural engineering program. I had taken the aptitude tests in high school, and all indications were that my strengths didn't lie in spatial design. But architecture sounded romantic, so I ignored the advice I had received in high school and enrolled in an architectural drawing class. It turned out to be a big mistake.

I retreated to the basement to do my homework after finishing my chores at the Trumbles. I finished most of my studying, then walked through the cold, deserted streets of Boulder back to the lab at the Architecture School. I was surrounded by self-assured architectural students as I sat hunched over the drawing board until midnight, plodding over my homework. It was hopeless; I still could muster only a grade of "D" in my architectural drawing class. I quickly realized the aptitude tests had been right; architecture was not my hidden talent.

Then there was the detachment from my friends. Although the North High crowd was all at CU, I was isolated in the Trumble's basement. With chores, babysitting and hours of architectural homework, I found no time for socializing. My only company was the radio and disc jockey Don Roberts on KOA.

I struggled, like most freshmen, to make the big adjustment to college life. I worried that my poor performance in architecture would threaten my scholarship, and I couldn't survive without it. I was isolated from my friends, and I had no one with whom I could share my fears. I didn't know that I was a normal freshman; in silence my classmates were all grappling with the same worries.

My first semester's woes were compounded by my living arrangements. Life in the Trumble basement was just one more failed attempt at bonding with a family, and I felt imprisoned by my duties at their home. I resented my isolation from campus and my high school cronies. I deplored every moment spent on chores because it took me away from my studies.

I plodded through the first semester, vowing to make some big changes to improve my college life when I returned for the second half of my freshman year.

Christmas vacation approached, and the air was filled with the excitement of homesick freshmen eager to return to the bosom of the family home. The atmosphere of gaiety choked me with loneliness as I realized I had nowhere to go. Once again, Jack Gershtenson came to my rescue, offering me remedy but not charity, which would have insulted my stubborn spirit. Mr. G. invited me back to the Home and gave me a job on the switchboard. I worked for my room and board.

When I returned to CU in January, I kept my promise and made big changes. I switched to the Arts and Sciences School with the idea of majoring in math. And I left the Trumbles and moved into the dormitory with my old pals, Charlie, Nate and Bernie.

I didn't have enough money for the meal plan in the dorm, so I got my meals by hashing in a girls' boarding house. My job was to serve the meals to about fifty girls and then clean up the dishes. I served three meals a day, six days a week. In exchange, I got a small paycheck and all the leftovers I could eat.

It was hard work, but the job took up only a small part of the day, leaving time for studying and socializing. It was a sharp and welcome contrast to life at the Trumbles where I was always on call. Liberated from the onus of late nights in the architectural lab, I was also better able to handle my course load. College life had taken a turn for the better.

While friends had parents to visit during vacations, I had the Home. Throughout my college years, the Home was like an anchor, providing stability in the rocky sea of college life. Not only did I operate the switchboard there every Sunday, but I also spent summers living and working at the Home as a recreational counselor.

Summers at the Home were idyllic. Freed from the grind of college exams and papers, I relished the relaxed outdoor life of carefree youth. I was responsible for supervising the young residents, but the work seemed like play. I could join the residents in games of softball on the lush Home grounds, go for a swim at a nearby rec center, or bowl alongside my young charges.

I was warmed by the summer sunshine and the affection of grateful kids, far from home and seeking someone with whom they could connect. I had a special empathy with the asthma patients in my charge because I had walked in their shoes. They felt my fondness and responded in kind.

Off-duty I savored the friendship of a tight-knit group of counselors. Most of them were college students from other states, and we lived on the Home grounds. Like me, the others had no place else to go on our days off, so we spent the time together. We became a transitory family. Together we visited Elitch's Amusement Park, where I tried to bury memories of dancing with Doris. We went shopping downtown and took brief forays into the mountains. I was always more comfortable with my peers than adults, and I embraced these summer kinships like a young child hugs his mother.

Strengthened by the friendships of summer life at the Home, I found the courage to dream about a college track career. I decided to write a letter to Coach Frank Potts asking him for advice. I sat at my desk in the Home dorm and anxiously scribbled a note to Coach Potts, telling him of my ambition to join the CU cross-country team. Then I waited eagerly for mail each day to see if he would reply. A few weeks later, my hopes were fulfilled. Potts wrote a polite, encouraging note, telling me to start my workouts and suggesting a daily routine.

I followed his counsel religiously. Every day when my obligations with the residents were fulfilled, I crossed the street to the junior high schoolyard and ran laps. I kept meticulous records of my times and strove to improve my record each night. I was determined to make a good showing.

I returned for my sophomore year at CU in great shape both physically and mentally. I could hardly wait to try out for the team. But it was not to be.

One morning, shortly after the fall semester began, I awoke with excruciating abdominal pain. I pulled on some clothes and staggered from my dorm room. I hobbled, doubled over in pain, to the Student Medical Center. I was immediately diagnosed with appendicitis and rushed by ambulance to the Boulder hospital. Before I knew what had hit me, I was in surgery and my afflicted appendix was removed. I lay in my hospital bed in a lonely stupor, weakened from the pain and the feeling of vulnerability. My spirits took a turn for the better, and my hopes returned through a fortuitous visit. My sister, Suzanne, and her boyfriend came up to Boulder to see me, and they spent hours trying to make me feel better. I laughed until my stitches were about to burst, and I regained my will to fight.

My recovery was long and frustrating. I walked bent like an arthritic old man around campus as I struggled to catch up on my coursework. Luckily now I was enrolled in math classes, where I had much more innate ability than in architecture, and it was less of a struggle to maintain good grades.

By the time I fully recovered from the appendicitis, it was too late for the cross-country season. My dream would have to wait for another year.

I returned to the Home the following summer and embarked on my daily workout routine with renewed vigor. This year, I vowed, nothing would keep me from trying out for cross-country. I could hardly wait for the summer to pass so I could get back to school and the tryouts.

I headed back to Boulder for my junior year, ready to leave the security of the dormitories. I arranged to share the top level of a house with two other guys: Red and Archie. Archie, a bright civil engineering major, had been a state wrestling champion in high school and was a member of the university team. Assertive and energetic, he encouraged me in my quest to join the cross-country team.

Finally, after more than a year of waiting for the cross-country tryouts, my big moment arrived. I was healthy, in great physical shape and mentally ready. The night before the time trials, I went to sleep early and slept well. I awoke in my apartment at dawn, impatient to get to the field. But I knew that I had to eat first. I set two pieces of white bread in the toaster and put a pot of water up to boil. When the toast popped, I slathered the two slices with honey, and dropped a Lipton teabag in a mug of hot water. I distractedly munched my toast, hoping this breakfast would be my good luck charm.

I headed over to Folsom Field, the university's football stadium, dressed in shorts and a T-shirt. I was filled with anticipation.

The September day was cool and overcast, and I took this as a good omen. It was my favorite running weather.

The cavernous stadium was empty except for the coach and the cross-country team hopefuls hovering near the starting line. I imagined the stands filled with fans watching me race around the track. I heard the roar of their thunderous applause and felt the sweat on my brow as I raced toward the finish line.

I quickly returned to reality as I approached my rivals, almost hidden in the vastness of the empty stadium. I counted my competitors — there were fifteen of us who dreamed of a place on the college team. Coach Potts scribbled down our names and posted a list on the scoreboard. He gave us instructions and announced he would accept the best seven. That meant I had to run faster than at least eight of the fit-looking collegiates gathered around Coach Potts to win a berth on the team.

The fifteen hopefuls stepped up to the starting line. My adrenalin pumped, and the blood rushed through my veins. I felt a mixture of intense anxiety and excitement. This was my big chance to prove myself as a competent athlete.

I looked upward into the overcast sky.

"Please God," I begged, "I just need to come in seventh. I want to make this team."

Potts blew the whistle, and we were off. I started around the quarter-mile track at a good pace and found myself in the middle of the pack. I concentrated on the muscles of my legs, urging them to go faster.

I looked around and saw that I was still in the middle as I began my twelfth lap. I realized that with a little extra effort, I had a good chance of making the team. I tapped the inner source of energy that had helped me survive the trials of my life. With a surge of power in my lanky legs, I whizzed past a Korean student who was at CU on a track scholarship. I rounded the finish line and dared to look up at the scoreboard. I was number seven. Euphoria permeated every sweaty pore of my body.

I, Eric Cahn, who had spent my life running from fear, hatred and neglect, had now run my way into success. I had actually made the University of Colorado cross-country team! Never before had I felt such a sense of accomplishment.

I rushed back home to tell my roommate Archie and to call Mr. G. with the news. My soul was suffused in sunlight on that cloudy Saturday. I immediately started a scrapbook and wrote on the first page, "These Were My Proudest Moments." A resident of the Home, Bill Grimes, later drew a colored-pencil rendition of me in runner's togs to grace the inside cover of the book.

The next weekend, I climbed in one of the University station wagons with the other team members and headed down to Norman, Oklahoma. The other team members were visibly surprised that I, an unknown, had made the team. But they were kindly encouraging, and the team spirit charged me with happiness.

When we arrived in Norman, each runner was assigned a number. The officials pinned the number eighteen on my chest. In Hebrew, eighteen is Chai, signifying life. And indeed, through running I had been reborn. Eric, the shy, out-of-place college boy, had found new meaning and new strength in life. The blood pumped through my body as I ran, feeding my starved soul with self-esteem.

Triggered by the energy of being on the team, I ran faster than ever before in Norman, but finished only twenty-fourth. Our team took second place, beat by Iowa State in the quadrangular meet that also included Oklahoma Baptist and Oklahoma University.

I spent four-and-a-half years at CU, and for my last three fall seasons, cross-country was the centerpiece of my life. I continued

*Eric's dream of athletic prowess came true! Eric, bottom right, was a member of
the 1959 varsity cross-country team at the University of Colorado.
Coach Frank Potts is in the top row, far left.*

to do well in my studies and work at the Home, but everything
else took a backseat to running.

My proudest moment came on April 25, 1959. Folsom Field
in Boulder was filled with spectators as competitors from Colorado and neighboring states arrived for the Colorado Relays.
That day, for the first time, I was asked to be part of the four-
man, four-mile relay team. I ran my best time ever, and our team
took the gold.

My scrapbook filled with news clippings as I diligently
perused the local papers and cut every article, whether positive
or negative, about our track and cross-country teams. The

changing fortunes of the team were reflected in the headlines, which ranged from "University Track Squad Sets Three New Records" to "Cross-Country Outlook is Bleak; Coach Potts Fears Finish in Basement."

I became a celebrity on Valentine's Day, 1959! *Rocky Mountain News* sports columnist Leonard Cahn, who called me "my namesake at Colorado," wrote about me in his column.

"Eric Cahn is built on the wiry side, 5-9 and 145 pounds, and has a crewcut and likes to run for the amusement of it," Cahn wrote. He revealed that I was a "displaced person" from Germany, but neither he nor I talked much about my past. My goal to be an all-American boy remained intact.

The college years passed quickly with running, work and school. Fall was filled with cross-country meets, and winter brought races with the track team. Each weekend was a new tomorrow, a chance to prove myself one more time. I pushed myself to new limits, slowly improving my race times. During my track career at CU, I earned two gold and two bronze medals.

I had come a long way. I started as an unknown who barely made the team and gradually earned the respect of the coach and my teammates. I was chosen to serve as captain for the cross-country team in my senior year. I had never felt so triumphant.

Cross-country even consumed my summers. Whenever I was off-duty from my counselor job at the Home, I worked out for track. For two summers, 1958 and 1959, a fellow counselor at the Home, JoAnne Fishlove, became my greatest fan and supporter. Each night after our chores were done, JoAnne and I crossed the street to Lake Junior High. JoAnne, armed with a stopwatch, timed my runs across the quarter-mile field. She kept fastidious notes about my times and my pulse rate.

My one-track mind was consumed by running, so I didn't realize that my relationship with JoAnne was budding into a romance. We began writing letters when she returned to college in Chicago after our second summer together. Cautiously we expressed our feelings through the shield of the written word.

After several months of flirting by mail, JoAnne wrote that she wanted to come out and watch me compete since she had been my trainer for two summers. My excitement grew as her trip neared, and suddenly I couldn't wait to see her.

JoAnne arrived in Denver on a cold, snowy weekend in February. The field house where we ran our indoor races was filled with fans, but I quickly found JoAnne's big brown eyes shining down on me. Fueled by her devotion, I ran a really good race, then raced to the showers and to JoAnne. We spent the night together in a hospital room at the Home, necking and talking. I felt our souls fuse and thought our future together was secure.

I had opened my heart for the first time since I lost Doris. I was like an uncorked bottle, spilling words of love into weekly letters. JoAnne responded in kind, and I couldn't wait to see her again.

When school ended that spring, I rushed to JoAnne's home in Chicago to pledge my love. She lived in an upper-middle-class suburb, and I was overwhelmed by the luxury of her parents' home, filled with fine bone china and heirloom-quality furniture. Although I was uncomfortable with their wealth, Mr. and Mrs. Fishlove treated me with enormous kindness. They were determined that I see Chicago, and the four of us went out for a night on the town. We ate dinner in a four-star downtown Chicago restaurant, then attended a stage performance of "Can Can."

I was filled with awe of the big city cultural life and love for JoAnne. I sneaked into JoAnne's bedroom after bidding her parents good night. Again, we stayed up all night talking and smooching, and I knew this was the real thing. I was in love.

JoAnne, however, had developed another relationship with a dental student in Chicago. She had invited me to Chicago to decide between the two of us. I refused to believe that she might be in love with the other man, and on my second night there, I proposed.

"I'm sorry, but I can't marry you, Eric," JoAnne said kindly. "I really believe I'm in love with this other man."

I was stricken with shock and sadness. I had already envisioned a long, happy future with JoAnne. Now she was telling me it was all over. I returned to the guest bedroom deflated by the sharp edge of rejection. The old hollowness in my stomach returned.

Sunday morning, I forlornly packed my bags. I couldn't wait to escape so I could be alone with my pain. Yet I hated leaving JoAnne. I was hardly able to hold my head up when I thanked her parents. I cried all the way back to Denver on the plane. Memories of my lonely plane ride from Copenhagen to the United States tore at my soul.

I replayed our talk over and over in my mind, trying to make it end differently. Stubbornness won over pride. I decided that I wouldn't give up; I would still try to win back JoAnne. I got back to the Home and rushed to the phone to make one final plea for her love. Maybe she had reconsidered after I left.

My fingers trembled as I dialed her phone number in Chicago. JoAnne answered, and I begged, "Please, JoAnne, think about it again. I love you and want to marry you."

JoAnne reaffirmed her commitment to the dental student. "I'm sorry Eric, I can't marry you," she said kindly, but firmly.

My heart dropped like a stone. I realized it was truly over. I never spoke to JoAnne again.

I went right back to work at the Home, this time promoted to the job of recreation director. With the speed of small-town gossip, the news of my rejected marriage proposal traveled fast. Everyone at the Home knew I was nursing a broken heart and treated me kindly.

I was apprehensive about starting any new relationships after the agonizing losses of Doris and JoAnne. I cautiously tested the waters by joking with Neva, a new medical secretary at the Home. I complimented her on her wonderful green eyes, and she flirted back. Bright and attractive, Neva took my mind off JoAnne's rejection. Neva was informally engaged to a drummer from Central City, a small mountain town that had faded from its glory as a center of the gold rush to a tourist trap with souvenir shops and funky bars. Later it would become one of Colorado's first legalized gambling centers. Neva's boyfriend offered a shield against a serious relationship. Or so I thought.

After two months of innocent flirting, I found the courage to ask Neva for a date. We went bowling, and she beat me badly. I took her home and shook her hand formally at the front door. She was engaged, after all, and I was a proper young man.

As the summer heat intensified, so did our flirting. Soon we were spending most evenings together, going to the movies or bowling. Neva broke off her engagement, and our relationship grew deeper, unfettered by other commitments. By the time summer was over, we were an item at the Home.

We continued to date after I returned to school in fall. She lived with two other women in an apartment in west Denver, a couple of miles west of the Home, and I often drove forty minutes from Boulder to be with her. On the weekends that I had cross-country races, she came up to Boulder to watch me run. We had good times together, and Neva made me laugh and forget about the losses of my past.

I shared little of my inner feelings or my past with Neva. She had learned bits and pieces of my history from working at the Home, but she never pried. I was still trying to forget where I had come from and live the American dream.

Neva's bubbly personality was the perfect antidote to my shyness. I could enjoy life vicariously through Neva. I was ready to graduate from college and eager to begin my adult life. And I desperately wanted to have children to recapture the childhood I had lost. I was as needy as a nursing pup, and I lapped up the chance for a normal family life with Neva.

One fall weekend, as the mountain aspens turned to gold, Neva and I drove up to Estes Park, a spectacular two-hour drive from Denver. We drove northwest on Highway 36 and got our first view of the small town, nestled in a mountain valley and surrounded by the lofty, jagged peaks of the Rocky Mountains. Towering majestically over the range was the snow-capped Longs Peak, at 14,255 feet one of Colorado's famous "fourteeners."

Estes Park is the gateway to Rocky Mountain National Park, sanctuary to elk and deer as well as millions of tourists each year. The natural attraction of the park had spawned man-made lures. Shrewd business people parlayed the park's popularity into successful commercial enterprises, and tourist traps lined Elkhorn Avenue, Estes Park's main street. Neva and I strolled arm-in-arm down the tourist-lined street, peering into a tawdry string of shops hawking salt-water taffy, cheap souvenirs and turquoise jewelry.

I was warmed by the splendor of the Continental Divide and Neva's high spirits. The moment had come. I guided Neva into a small jewelry store. We picked out a gold ring with a black onyx stone, and I carefully placed it on her finger. We were engaged.

Chapter Nine

Family Man

I awoke on the morning of Sunday, January 29, 1961, with a knot in my stomach. Alone in the ground floor apartment that Neva and I had rented in west Denver, I pushed through the clouds of sleepiness fogging my mind. My head instantly cleared when I realized the root of my anxiety — it was my wedding day. I showered and shaved in a trance, mechanically going through the motions while my thoughts traveled into the future with a mixture of excitement and fear.

I carefully shook the plastic wrapping off the rented black tuxedo, laid the jacket on the bed and put my arms through the sleeves of the snow-white shirt. Snapping the black velvet bowtie into place, I struggled to keep my hands from shaking. I was taking on the responsibilities of married life with little experience to guide me. What did I, the war orphan, know about how to live a happy, normal, American family life?

I was jittery as a teen on his first date as I closed the door on my bachelorhood and headed for the chapel. I carefully maneuvered the 1958 chartreuse T-bird, borrowed from Neva's brother, west along Colfax Avenue, a commercial street filled with retail shops. I headed toward the modest Chapel of the Angels wedding hall, sandwiched between a row of stores. I steered past Leon the Neon giraffe, advertising the adjacent furniture store, and made a tight right turn into the chapel parking lot.

Neva, already at the chapel in her stunning white gown, was in a state of panic. The maid of honor's gown hadn't been delivered to the chapel as promised. Neva made a series of phone calls, finally reaching the night watchman at the May Company, one of downtown Denver's finest department stores, where she had purchased the dress. The watchman came to the rescue and tracked down the dress. It arrived just before the ceremony, and the maid of honor hurriedly got dressed.

Finally all was ready. Neva's father sobbed as he escorted his only daughter, not quite twenty-one, down the aisle. Since Neva was Christian and I, a nonpracticing Jew, we decided to exchange vows in a civil ceremony. We were married by a stranger, a justice of the peace provided by the chapel. I went through the ceremony in a daze, and before I knew what happened, I was a married man.

The fog stayed in my head through the reception where we served punch and wedding cake to our friends. Neva had some visiting aunts, and we had invited a number of friends from the Home. The director at the Home had wanted to make the wedding a big publicity stunt, but I would have no part of it. Parties made me uneasy, and I wanted the ordeal to be over as quickly as possible.

We were surrounded by Neva's family and friends, yet I felt scared and alone. Once again I was journeying into foreign territory without family to support me. My only close relative, my sister, Suzanne, had gone into labor and was in the hospital. Neva and I were exchanging vows while Suzanne was awaiting the arrival of her firstborn.

Our duties at the reception were finally fulfilled, and Neva and I made our escape. We dressed in our traveling clothes, and headed for the T-bird and Colorado Springs. I had paid in advance for two nights at the posh Broadmoor Hotel. The honeymoon suite had cost me dearly — thirty-five dollars a night — and we couldn't wait to treat ourselves to our first taste of luxury.

We settled into our luxurious digs and were relishing the comforts of the Broadmoor when the ringing phone shattered our privacy. It was Neva's mother, calling to report that Suzanne had delivered twins. We abandoned the Broadmoor early the next morning. Our honeymoon was brought to a premature close as I drove the T-bird straight to the hospital to meet my new nephews.

I peered at my sister's twin sons through the glass windows of the nursery and was awed by the feelings of love they evoked. Here was the promise of the future, a hope for a better tomorrow. I too wanted children, and I wanted them immediately.

I was only twenty-three and weeks out of college, but I was impatient to get on with adult life. Neva didn't resist my desire for instant parenthood. She became pregnant immediately while we settled into married life in our apartment in west Denver. We both continued to work at the Home that summer. I began teaching in the fall, and Neva stayed home to finish out the final stages of her pregnancy.

Neva went into labor late on a snowy October evening. I drove cautiously down the ice-covered streets of west Denver, and it seemed like hours before we reached the emergency doors at St. Anthony's Hospital, just a couple of miles northeast of home. Neva was taken off to the labor room, and I was left behind in a state of nervous anticipation. I paced the quiet linoleum halls of the hospital awaiting news of my first child's birth. After what seemed like days, I was face to face with the doctor.

"Congratulations, Mr. Cahn. You have a daughter. Mother and baby are doing fine," he said, smiling and shaking my hand.

I rushed to the nursery and stared at our tiny baby, Patricia Michelle, in reverence. I could hardly believe my good fortune. My dream of fatherhood had come true. Here was living proof of my survival!

It was early morning, October 8, 1961, and my life was changed forever. I was a father first from that day forward. I lavished my affections on my child at the cost of all others, especially Neva. I silently swore that Patti would not lack for anything, including my abiding affection. As a doting parent, I could find the childhood I had lost. I didn't realize that by giving my undivided devotion to my child, I was slowly eroding my marriage.

Unfortunately, Patti was a difficult baby. She cried constantly the first year, no matter what we tried. We spent our days in the waiting rooms of countless doctors, but none could recommend a cure for her distress. We took Patti for tests at Children's Hospital in desperation. But despite the persistent pricking and poking of pediatric specialists, they too failed to find the cause for her constant discomfort.

Neva and I, resigned to sleep deprivation, took turns getting up and trying to soothe our restless babe. We tried ignoring her on the advice of the more stern doctors. Finally we bought earplugs that we inserted each night to shut out Patti's incessant cries.

One night Patti's howls shook us from sleep, and we decided to give her a bottle. Neva staggered to the kitchen and set the bottle in a pan of water to heat. She and I fell fast asleep with the bottle on the stove. Fifteen minutes later, we awoke to an apartment filled with smoke. We had burned out all the water, and the pan was red hot. We realized that sleep deprivation was tearing at the edges of sanity, and our very safety was at stake. So we continued to seek a miracle cure for our inconsolable baby.

When Patti was almost a year old, Neva was taking her for a walk and passed a new doctor's office. Neva was desperate for help, so she went in and spilled her guts about the troubles we were having. His diagnosis was that all the medications we had given Patti were working in reverse, and he took her off everything but Benadryl. She miraculously started sleeping through the night within a month.

With sanity finally restored, Neva and I decided to have a second child. We both desperately wanted a son, and we didn't want to leave it to chance. Neva had become good friends with our next door neighbor, Peggy Marks, and discussed our desires with her. Peggy had read a number of books on how to predict the gender of your baby, and she advised Neva that a certain time of the month was best to conceive boys.

So we went to work. Neva carefully kept a calendar and counted the days. One night, when I got home from work, Neva told me the time was right. This was the night to conceive a son.

I wanted to be well-prepared for the evening, so I decided to shave. I went in the bathroom, only to discover I was out of razor blades. I knocked on Peggy's door to borrow a razor blade, and she grinned from ear to ear, surmising exactly what was happening at our house. I blushed as I thanked her for the blade and headed home. Neva conceived that evening, and we waited eagerly for the birth of our second child.

Peggy's trick worked! Jeff came into the world on December 7, 1963, as I watched football in the St. Joseph's Hospital waiting room. Like a spectator at a tennis match, my attentions were divided. I bounced nervously from the labor room to check Neva and back to the waiting room to check the football scores. I couldn't stand the tension of Neva's labor pains, and I was relieved when it was finally over.

As I stared into my infant son's eyes, my own brimmed with tears of joy. We had a son and a daughter, and my dreams of a family were reality. I renewed my pledge to keep my children safe and fill their lives with love and hope.

Neva was as euphoric as I was. I rolled her out of the delivery room, and she asked me to stop at a pay phone in the hall. Our neighbor Peggy had moved to California, and Neva wanted to call her immediately to tell her the trick had worked.

Neva's life was overtaken by bottles and diapers. Her days were a whirlwind of child care, and I did little to ease her burden. Driven by the need to prove myself as a worthy provider, I was rarely home. Instead I crammed work into every corner of my time.

By day, I taught at Smiley Junior High, at 26th and Holly, earning a respectable $4,575 a year. Smiley was in a typical east Denver neighborhood of brick bungalows. The neighborhood had been home to the white middle class, and now more African-American families had begun to move in. My students represented the diversity of the changing neighborhood.

We had moved to a duplex less than a mile from Smiley, and I went home from work for a quick bite to eat. Then I headed up to Boulder, a forty-minute commute, to work on my master's degree in school administration at the University of Colorado. Weekends, I supplemented our income by working at the Home.

The treadmill of my life had begun to take its toll even before Jeff was born, and I started to have serious migraine headaches. One headache was particularly memorable. I was teaching algebra to ninth graders the afternoon of November 22,

1963, while Neva was still pregnant with Jeff. I was trying desperately to fight off the pain that racked my head. Our class was interrupted by a somber voice over the school's announcement system.

"We have a serious announcement to share with you about something that just occurred. President Kennedy was shot and killed in a Dallas motorcade," the disembodied voice said.

My eyes filled with tears as I stared unseeing out the

Eric the teacher behind his desk at Smiley Junior High in 1962. His career in education was short-lived since he soon took the opportunity to work at the Home.

large, west-facing windows of my second-story classroom. The students and I were stunned into silence.

"How could this be?" I mused in sullen sadness. Kennedy was my hero. The 1960 election had been my first opportunity to vote, and I proudly had cast my ballot for Kennedy. I worshipped the young, charismatic president and the promise he had represented. Suddenly my world was turned upside down, and my headache seemed insignificant.

I turned to face the dazed students, and we began to talk in whispers. "Why did this happen? How could it happen?" we asked as we tried to make sense of the senseless act.

The rest of the weekend was a roller coaster of emotion as Neva, rotund in her ninth month of pregnancy with Jeff, and I, like the rest of America, stayed glued to the television. We watched as Air Force One brought our fallen president home, and we cried as John John saluted his father's casket. It was a weekend I'd never forget.

The Kennedy assassination bonded me to my students, but teaching soon became a chore. I felt imprisoned by the four walls of the classroom and the repetitive routine of six class periods a day. I thought the best escape was to complete my studies and vie for a position as a school principal.

I quickly learned the hard lessons of school politics. I wasn't savvy enough to play the social games necessary to win the principal's favor. Although I was hired at the same time as a number of other young teachers, they soon passed me by. While they got honors classes, I continued to get the disagreeable classes and undesirable schedules.

I was unable to succeed in the social arena, so I decided the way to prosper was to work harder. I conscientiously wrote lesson plans each night after I returned from my graduate school classes. And I established an after-school math team to win my principal's approbation.

The team was popular, and fifteen boys and girls joined me in my classroom weekly after school to explore math concepts. It was the time of the infamous "new math," and one of our challenges was to demonstrate the binary system. The students and I designed a crude binary computer, replete with flashing colored lights that could be turned on and off. The energetic group of math lovers provided an oasis in the endless desert of my teaching days.

I made some attempts to be part of the school social scene, and I agreed to play Santa Claus for the students at an after-school party. I sweated inside the big red suit as I walked up and down the aisles of the auditorium handing out candies.

Jeff and Patti (Michelle) as toddlers. Eric's children became the center of his life as he tried to redress the childhood he had lost.

I managed to get average evaluations for my teaching skills, and after three years, Principal Marvin Powell recommended me for tenure. I continued to work on my master's in school administration, hoping to become a principal some day.

I continued to spend summers at the Home as recreation director. As summer approached, I looked forward to the freedom of the outdoors, a break from the tedium of the classroom.

I had my first taste of supervision as recreation director overseeing the staff of college students who served as counselors, the same job I had filled for four years during my college days. I learned, much to my surprise, that I was a natural supervisor. The hard work I modeled was followed by my subordinates, and my enthusiasm for the Home was contagious.

Mr. G. watched my growth with the pride of a loving father. When a full-time, permanent position came open at the Home, he actively recruited me.

Chapter Ten

Back Home

In the spring of 1964, Mr. G. approached me with an offer. "Eric, how would you like to come back to the Home full-time?" Mr. G. asked. He chomped on his ever-present cigar as we sat in his office where I had made so many requests as a youth.

"We need a new director of residential programs, and I think you're ready for the job," he assured me.

Although I had just been offered tenure at Smiley Junior High, it took only seconds to think over the offer. I couldn't refuse. The job would free me from the monotony of the classroom, give me more responsibility, and let me repay a debt to the Home.

Mr. G. described the demanding job he was asking me to accept. The Home had grown since I had lived there, and as director of residential programs, I would be responsible for the day-to-day lives of 150 asthmatic children. Only their medical care and the kitchen would be outside my purview. I would also get the chance to supervise, hire and fire a staff of more than thirty-five college students and adults.

I went home and told Neva about the offer. She agreed it was a great opportunity, and I accepted the job. I immediately began spending evenings and weekends back at the Home to learn about my new duties.

I could hardly wait for the school year to end. I taught my last weeks of class and finished grading finals. When the last day of school arrived, I turned in my final grades, packed up my few personal belongings and said goodbye to my career in teaching.

I was ready for a new challenge. The next day, I arrived in my office at the Home at 7:30 a.m., eager to begin my quest to improve life for the young residents. My office was located in the Simon Building, where I had lived as a teen. The east side of the building, formerly the girls' dorms, had been converted to a hospital, replacing the aging infirmary. The west wing, where I had lived, was now offices.

My modest office was a converted bedroom. The small, square room had only a desk and phone. The closet space had been altered to serve as storage shelves. Barely disguised as an office, the old dorm room flooded me with memories and gratitude. I was determined to make the Home a better place and return the favors Jack Gershtenson had showered on me over the years.

Mr. G. had warned me that my initial duties would be difficult ones. He explained that my predecessor had allowed some incompetent people to remain on staff, and it would be my job to get rid of them.

I was only twenty-six, and the first thing I had to do was fire a sixty-five-year-old houseparent who didn't work well with the residents. It was the hardest thing I had ever done, but I knew the welfare of my young charges was at stake. I gathered up my courage and told the man that he had to leave.

That difficult chore completed, I had to hire a new house-parent. But before I could make a decision, I needed to know more about the job. I called a meeting of the houseparents and learned that they had no written expectations.

"How can you perform a job if you don't know what the requirements are?" I asked rhetorically. Together we developed a job description.

As we wrote down all they did each day, I came to appreciate how difficult and demanding their jobs were. The house-parents took care of the kids from the time they got up at seven each morning until they went to bed at nine each night. The houseparents were surrogate parents, and their days were crammed with meeting the physical, emotional and mental needs of the residents. Many of our children were severe asthma cases, and the houseparents had to deal with life-and-death crises at all hours of the day and night.

The houseparents received room and board, and a very modest salary in exchange for five days of round-the-clock duty. It was a stressful job, and we lost many staff members to burn-out.

I realized how hard they worked and how little they were appreciated by the Behavior Science staff. It soon became my mission to reduce turnover by improving the lot of the house-parents. I was their champion with the Home's top administration. I fought for salary increases and worked on scheduling so they could get two consecutive days off each week. I also struggled to enhance their reputation with the doctors and psychologists who treated them like second-class citizens. The house-parents returned my devotion with loyalty and dedication.

Being at the Home was like returning to the womb. I drove to the Home each day, feeling I was truly going back to the place of my birth as a mature adult. The Home had given me the confidence to go off into the world, and now I was returning to help other youngsters flourish.

Memories of my lonely youth were still fresh, and I was as committed to enriching the lives of the residents as I was to helping the houseparents. I sat in my dormitory-room-turned-office, drifting back in time to my years at the Home to uncover what would have made a difference in my teen years.

One of my most poignant recollections was the loneliness of the holidays. The residents, far away from home and living in an institution, felt more isolated and homesick than ever when the holiday season arrived. I tried to think of some ways I could ease the pain of being far from family during the holidays.

My staff and I came up with a brainstorm. Why not develop a "home away from home" program for the residents? Rather than have them eat Thanksgiving turkey in the austere, institutional dining room, why not place them in family settings? We contacted the local churches and synagogues, and we asked their members to volunteer to take a resident home for the holidays.

Placing 150 asthmatic children was a logistical challenge, but we found a family for every child. The program became a huge success with the residents, who reveled in the warmth of a family celebration. Their parents, relieved that their children were with surrogate families, filled my mailbox with notes of gratitude.

I also remembered the monotony of summer days as a resident confined to the hospital grounds. While we had play fields and activities at the Home, the summer days loomed long without school as a distraction. The few small acres that the Home filled became a prison of boredom when the residents were sequestered there day after day. I thought they needed a change of scenery.

I cajoled the kitchen staff, and finally they agreed to help with weekly summer cookouts for the kids at local parks. Each week we loaded residents on the Home's old school bus and took them to nearby Sloan's Lake for an outing. The change of scenery was an antidote for the ennui of the summer days.

I also believed the residents needed more opportunities to become physically strong. The children participated in swimming, bowling, baseball, horseback riding, volleyball and more, but we had never tried competitive activities. I made an appointment with Dr. Hyman Chai, the chief clinician.

"Dr. Chai, the Lakewood Jaycees, a local service club, has formed a flag football league, and I'd like to start a team from the Home to compete," I said.

Dr. Chai pondered the request. "It's something we've never tried before, but perhaps it will work. We'll try it for a while and if the boys can do it and stay healthy, we'll let them participate. If it's too strenuous, we'll have to withdraw," Chai said.

I went back to the dorms and put out a call for team members. The response was immediate and enthusiastic. The boys, ages ten to twelve, couldn't wait to test their strength against healthy Denver kids. The "Asthmatic Eleven" was born. With close medical supervision, the boys practiced after school a couple of days each week. Two of the houseparents, Tom Blowers and Jack Leonard, served as coaches.

We packed the team and any fans we could round up on the Home's old school bus each Saturday afternoon and headed over to the Lakewood High School fields, a suburban stadium a few miles west of the home. I joined several of the houseparents to cheer the boys on. I marveled at the boys as they raced around the field with the blue or red flags hanging from their pockets. Some boys had to use their nebulizers, breathing devices for asthmatics, during halftime, but they'd return to the field ready for the game.

The sweet smell of victory was ours week after week as the boys tore the flags from their opponents' pockets. The young residents on the sidelines jumped up and down with glee, unable to contain themselves as our team racked up the points. For the moment they could ignore their own fragile health. It was easy to forget that some of these children had come to Colorado as a last-ditch effort to save their lives.

We ended our first season with six wins, one tie and no defeats. We had won the championship of our eight-team league! The officers of the Lakewood Jaycees came to the Home, and in a special ceremony in our dining hall, presented each team member with a trophy. It was a moment of triumph for the Home, Dr. Chai, the boys and me. We had proven these sickly children could benefit from competitive sports, and could compete effectively.

Our victories brought headlines in both the *Denver Post* and the *Rocky Mountain News*. A *Medical Tribune* report in 1966 marveled at the success of our asthmatic athletes. "Hospital records show that most of the players were so seriously ill with asthma before coming to CARIH (Children's Asthmatic Research Institute and Hospital, the new name for the Home) that even walking to school was impossible. Some were almost bedfast," the article noted. Now they were flag football champs!

Flushed with our success at flag football and our relationship with the Jaycees, I sought help from other service clubs as well. Their reception was warm, and many groups eagerly contributed to enrich life for the youngsters at the Home. In 1965, the *Rocky Mountain News* featured a picture of our residents and me playing pool on a table donated by the B'nai B'rith. The

Denver Post had a photo of us getting tickets to a hockey game from a college fraternity.

I was working to the point of exhaustion, but I kept striving to do more. I knew I was making a difference in the lives of the residents in a way that only someone who had walked in their shoes could. The youngsters treated me like a family member, and parents who came to visit always stopped by my office to thank me for nurturing their children.

Officially I worked five-and-a-half days a week, but I usually went to the Home on Sunday mornings too, often taking Patti and Jeff with me. I saw my twelve-hour days as a small token of repayment to the Home and Mr. G. for years of support. The Home had helped create Eric Cahn, and I couldn't seem to do enough in return.

Some of the residents came to us not only with health problems, but also with behavioral problems. I was on call every night, and when our phone rang at 11:00 p.m., I jumped out of bed, knowing there was trouble at the Home. Bedtime at the Home had come and gone, and a ten-year-old boy was missing, the frantic houseparent on the other end of the line reported.

I pulled on my jeans and sweater and rushed out the door. The fifteen-minute car ride seemed endless as I anxiously planned my mode of attack. I parked the car and headed underground to the tunnels that connected the old buildings — the hospital, Lorber Building, Boys Building and Willens Building. These tunnels joined the canteen, storage rooms and playrooms and were a favorite hideout for homesick young boys.

I darted around a corner in the tunnel and spotted a bent figure huddled against the cold. I sat down next to him and, hiding the anxiety his antics had caused me, calmly asked what was going on.

"The houseparent yelled at me," the young boy sobbed.

I listened with empathy to win his trust. Not trained as a counselor, I didn't attempt to solve his problems. Instead, my job was to calm him down enough to get him back to the dorm. In the morning we would make an appointment with the Behavior Sciences staff to work on his psychological needs.

The boy seemed ready to take my advice after a few more minutes of weeping.

"Everything will seem better in the morning if you get a good night's sleep," I told the tired, scared young boy. Together, we walked out of the tunnel and back to the dorm. I handed the youngster over to the relieved houseparent and headed for home.

I took a deep breath as I turned the key in the ignition of my car. Another near-tragedy averted. A few short hours later, I was back at the Home for another day's work.

Occasionally, my tunnel searches were unsuccessful, and I paced the grounds looking for the runaways. If all the old haunts came up empty, I had no choice but to call the police. The Denver Police Department was familiar with the Home, and they would respond quickly. Usually, they found the youngsters wandering the neighborhood nearby. I never did have to call parents, hundreds of miles away, to report their child AWOL.

Some nights I voluntarily went to the Home in the wee hours without an emergency to bring me there. I set the alarm for 2:00 a.m., got up in the dark and quickly dressed and drove over to the Home to check up on the night attendants. Mostly women in their sixties from east Denver, they worked the 10:00 p.m. to 6:00 a.m. shift. They were supposed to stay up all night in case a child got sick.

I arrived at the Home in the middle of the night and walked furtively into the cottage lounge to make sure the night attendants were awake. Occasionally, I caught someone dozing and had to shake her by the shoulder. Most nights, however, I returned home to bed secure in the fact that we had reliable night attendants who were doing their jobs. I never fired one.

Another part of my job was making sure the residents got to the appropriate religious services. Although the Home had a Jewish heritage, there were as many as fifteen religions represented at the Home at any one time.

We had our own rabbi, Nate Davidovich's father, who supervised the kosher kitchen. Mr. Davidovich held Hebrew classes and Friday night services in the basement of the Willens Building. We also sponsored catechism classes and Sunday services for the Catholic students in that room.

The rest of our residents went to neighborhood churches. When a resident came to the Home, we talked to the parent about religious preferences. It was then my job to make arrangements with the local church of that denomination.

Sunday mornings after breakfast, our residents dressed in their best clothes and came out to the front entrance to wait for their rides. Parishioners from the neighborhood churches pulled into the driveway in a steady stream to pick up our young charges and take them to church. The system worked, and we never lost a child or sent him off to the wrong church.

While the children's asthmatic condition was treated on-site by the medical staff, as surrogate parents we had to coordinate all their other medical needs. I developed relationships with local dentists and optometrists to serve our residents. One young dentist, Stanley Gottlieb, came to the Home every Wednesday, his day off, to treat the residents on grounds free of charge. I had never been to a dentist before he treated me as a fifteen-year-old resident of the Home, and he spent hundreds of unpaid hours caring for my long-neglected teeth. I still go to him today.

Not only did I coordinate all the programs, but I also had to perform my own clerical duties, often late in the evening after all the other day's work was done. I was not a very good typist, and I would slowly peck away at the typewriter, seething in frustration as I crumbled page after page of mangled letters. I fought with the typewriter for a year before I pleaded with Mr. G. for help. He agreed to let me hire a secretary.

In 1965 I hired Pauline Duffy, who became my greatest fan and confidante. Office space was at a premium, and Pauline had to sit in a corner of the hallway of the Simon Building, a few yards from my converted dorm room office.

Pauline was just returning to the work force after staying at home to raise her children for seventeen years. She was eager to do a good job and took a brush-up course in typing and shorthand. Pauline immediately became a member of the Home family, serving as a mother figure to the residents and a best friend to me. She surprised me with a cupcake replete with candle for my birthday and a congratulatory card when good things came my way. When I was frustrated with work at the Home, Pauline provided a shoulder to cry on. I was grateful for her simple gifts of caring.

As a perfectionist, I was a demanding boss. I dictated a memo to Pauline, and she quickly typed it for me, making a carbon copy for my records. I reviewed her work with a fine-tooth comb and sent her back to retype anything with a dirt smudge or the smallest error. Pauline returned to her typewriter without a word of protest to redo the memo countless times until I found it suitable for my signature.

Pauline was in daily contact with parents of the residents. She empathized as a mother and knew how hard it was for them to be hundreds of miles from their sickly children. Her calm, reassuring voice told parents all over the United States that their children were in good hands.

The Home became a family affair for the Duffys. Pauline volunteered to take Vicky Jo, a spunky little girl with Shirley Temple curls, home for the holidays. Although Vicky was a hellion at the Home, she was an angel for Pauline.

I hired Pauline's daughter, Patricia, to work on the recreation staff in the summer of 1967. She met Jim Andersen, a recreation counselor from Loveland, Colorado, and they fell in love. They married the next summer with eighty of the Home's residents in attendance. I arranged for Vicky Jo to return home to New York a few days late so she could be a junior attendant at the wedding.

With Pauline at my side, the workload became more bearable. But I was still working almost seven days a week in my eternal quest to better serve the residents.

I was flushed with my triumphs, and I wanted to take on more projects unfettered by the medical bureaucracy. The Home was a medical institution first, and there was an unspoken caste system. The medical staff was at the top of the pyramid, and the rest of us were treated like second-class serfs. The doctors and psychologists showed little understanding or respect for the work we did with the residents. They acted as if we were there to serve their needs. While I envisioned a partnership, they expected unchallenged servility.

I was often stopped short by the whims of the doctors and Behavior Sciences staff. I viewed these people as cold and distant, at the Home from nine to five to do a job, but not really caring about the residents as needy children.

I was weary of this second-class treatment by January 1968, after four years at the home. I wrote a "New Year's Message" to express my disgust with the "professional" staff. The houseparents and I declared 1968 the "Year of Enlightenment" and proclaimed, "We will no longer tolerate the aura of subservience which has existed for so many years... We are frankly very tired of being pushed around and having the buck passed to us ... We will not sit back and be appeased...."

We demanded that the title be changed from "houseparent" to "counselor" and that professional staff members address us as "Mr., Miss or Mrs." in front of the children and in written communications.

I fired off the memo to Dr. Constantine Falliers, the new medical director. Days, then weeks passed, and we heard nothing. It was like our memo had fallen into a black hole. After waiting for several months, I went to see Mr. G.

"I'm going to make an appointment with Dr. Falliers. If he doesn't agree to our demands, I'll threaten to quit," I told Mr. G.

He raised his eyebrows in surprise and stared into my eyes, pondering how to respond. He knew I was stubborn and impatient. This was not the first time he had tried to tighten the reins while I had tried to bolt through the unwritten rules of the professional establishment.

Mr. G. examined me across his desk, biting hard on the inevitable cigar.

"Take a vacation with your family, Eric. You are exhausted from four years of hard work without a break. Get away from here for a couple of weeks, and you'll see things in a different light," Mr. G. suggested in a fatherly tone.

I shook my head, rejecting his idea, and rose from my chair with impatience. He was trying to warn me about what was ahead, but I refused to hear him. I was ready for a showdown. Like a labor leader fighting for his workers' rights, I would accept no compromise.

It was a warm day in May, five months after I had sent the ultimatum, that I went to see Dr. Falliers. I marched up the steps of the Research Building like a young man going to war.

Falliers was a bright, good-looking man in his forties. He had been a Fulbright Scholar, and he was the consummate diplomat. He hated conflict and avoided confrontation.

He greeted me warmly and asked me to take a seat in front of his desk.

I took a deep breath and calmly began. "I want things to change for my people or I will resign my position. We have to be treated with more respect as we stated in the January memo."

Falliers didn't take my bait. He refused to make any promises about conditions for the houseparents and responded coolly to my threat.

"If you feel that you must leave the Home, Eric, we will be sorry to lose you. But I will understand," he said without a trace of emotion.

I skulked out of his office, shoulders sagging with defeat. I had let my people down, had played my trump card and lost. I saw no choice but to make good on my vow.

On May 15, I made my resignation official through a letter. My resignation was effective October 1, but with a month's vacation coming, I planned to leave September 1.

The last few months at the Home spun by in a dream filled with regret. These had been the most rewarding four years of my life, and I was sorry to see them end. But I was tired of fighting the bureaucracy, and I was worn out.

I spent the last week training my replacement, a houseparent who was to be promoted. I was filled with trepidation when I tried to spill my brain into his. He had not experienced life at the Home as I had, and I saw neither the talent nor the high level of commitment. I was afraid all my hard work would crumble. On my last day, I followed my regular routine, marching into the west end of the dining hall with the 150 residents for the last time. The sound of chairs scraping across the linoleum filled the cavernous room as the residents settled into their seats. Each residential cottage had its own long table, and a cart with kosher food sat at the end waiting to be served. The summer sun streamed into the windows from the north and south, filling the room with warmth. The room grew still for the traditional moment of silence.

Instead of the usual rush for the food though, the room remained still after the moment of silence had passed. Then a young boy approached me, his outstretched hands holding a small gift box.

"This is a gift for you to remember us by," the ten-year-old lad said.

My hands shook, as taken totally by surprise, I opened the box. Inside was a silver Hamilton watch with six diamonds on its face. On the back, it read, "Eric Cahn, for his devotion and service to asthmatic children, from the boys and girls at CARIH, 1968."

My eyes brimmed with tears as I choked out a few words of thanks.

"I will miss being with you boys and girls," I sobbed. "It has meant so much to me to be involved in your lives."

I sat down, and the room filled with applause. I passed through the rest of the day in a fog. I had chosen this separation, yet it was creating another major loss in my life. The children of the Home had filled me with love and a reason for being. They had given me a chance to prove myself and to repay old debts. The Home had been a better tomorrow, and now I had to leave its womb once again.

I was now out on the streets with two children and a wife to support. Mr. G. came to the rescue one more time, helping me find a job as activity director for the Jewish Community Center, a nonprofit organization that offered social, cultural and recreational activities to community members of all ages and faiths although strongly Jewish in focus.

Chapter Eleven

A Chance to Shine

While my career was progressing and enriching my life,
Neva had little contact with the outside world, and
she craved some social opportunities.

A neighbor in Lakewood was president of the Lakewood
Jaycees, an organization for young men between the ages of
twenty-one and thirty-six that encouraged leadership training
through community involvement. Neva became good friends
with the president's wife, and learned about the women's auxiliary, the Jaycee Ettes, which offered her the promise of new
friends and activities. Neva cajoled me into joining the Jaycees
because she yearned to be a member of the women's auxiliary.

I was not eager to join. I still felt like a greenhorn in social
settings, and I avoided large groups. But to keep the peace at
home, I started attending meetings. During my first year, I stood
at the perimeter, observing but not participating.

My life as a Jaycee took a dramatic turn after a Christmas party in 1964 at the home of Chapter President Seary Nicoli. Seary lived in a two-story house on a typical suburban street in Lakewood. By the time we drove up to his house for the party, the street was lined with Fords and Chevys, and I couldn't find a close place to park. I yearned to turn around and go home, but I knew Neva would hear nothing of it. I cruised farther down the block of identical homes and pulled into the first available spot.

We hurried up the street to Seary's home, and I huddled against the cold and my dread of what was to come. Parties were a special kind of torture for me. A loner who had never had many friends, I anticipated social events like a visit to the dentist. Pain and discomfort were my only expectations. I bolstered myself for several hours of sheer misery, knowing Neva would be in her prime and eager to stay as late as possible. I would endure.

The party was in the basement, a large, pine-paneled recreation room dressed up with Christmas decorations and an ornament-laden tree. The centerpiece of the room was a long wooden table crammed with chips and dip, cold cuts, punch and beer. The food was like a magnet, and about forty Jaycees and their wives gathered around to fill their plates. In the background, mellow dance music played, and a few couples did a slow waltz.

My spirits deflated as the decibel level swelled. Drowning in a sea of small talk, I sought safe harbor in a quiet corner. I stood silently against the wall, feeling like a sailor shipwrecked in a foreign land.

Gregarious Neva bubbled buoyantly from one conversation to another, oblivious to my torment. It was through a stranger's eyes that Neva finally saw me for who I was. Neva was talking to the unknown Jaycee when his eyes caught sight of me in the corner.

Pointing in my direction, he said, "Who is that guy in the corner, looking like he's lost?" Neva had to admit it was her husband, and the incident ruined her evening.

On the way home, Neva sat on her side of the car, not saying a word. The chill of her anger froze the air in the car.

Finally I asked, "Is something wrong? What happened at the party?"

"I was embarrassed by your behavior, standing in the corner like a lost child," Neva said, recounting the callous stranger's comments.

"Was it that obvious that I felt out of place?" I asked rhetorically, realizing instantly how I appeared to the rest of the club.

My gorge filled with the sour taste of anger and humiliation. I swallowed hard and resolved that by the next Christmas party, every member of the Lakewood Jaycees would know Eric Cahn. I took this incident as a challenge to my manhood rather than admit defeat as a social failure. Vater and Oma had belittled me; I would not allow some strangers to join the torment. I would prove myself by hard work.

The party was an impetus to action, and by mid-1965, I was involved in a number of committees, spending most of my precious spare time with the Jaycees.

Meanwhile, the Jaycee Ettes became the defining focus of Neva's life. An outgoing, bright woman, she was isolated at home with our two babies. Now she had found a release for her pent-up social needs. Neva was eager to participate in the "Speak Up" competition, a speech contest. She convinced me to go with her to our first state meeting in the summer of 1965 in Estes Park, the romantic mountain town where we had gotten engaged. She took second place in the state competition. Neva was flying high, and as her involvement grew, she urged me to take a leadership role.

I decided I could manage a position of power after much prodding. In 1967 I became vice president of our Lakewood chapter and state membership chairman. We had the highest membership ever, almost 4,000 statewide, and I found to my surprise that I liked organizing and managing events for the Jaycees.

I was flushed with my success and decided to make a bid for the presidency of the Lakewood Jaycees in 1968. We had 110 members, and I had tough competition in the form of Marlin Fisher, a veteran member who was supported by many of the club's old-timers.

I set up a campaign team, and with the stamina of a long-distance runner, I began a tireless effort toward victory. I brought a mixture of stubbornness, determination and compulsive hard work to the task. I established a campaign committee, and we brainstormed a slogan, MA over LT — more action, less talk. We passed out MA/LT buttons to the membership, and the campaign picked up steam. I went into the election night meeting fully expecting success.

The election was held the evening of March 20, 1968, during our regular meeting in the basement of Bank Western in Lakewood. We had a written ballot because there were two candidates. The assembled members wrote their choice for the next president in secret. The election committee ceremoniously collected the ballots and went off in the corner to count them.

My campaign team and I waited impatiently for the results, trying to bide the time with the kind of small talk that made me so uncomfortable. The vote tallying seemed to take forever. The announcement came at 9:40 p.m. I was victorious! Eric Cahn, who a few years earlier was an awkward loner hidden in the corner of a Jaycees Christmas party, was now president of the 110-

member organization. I had reached my goal; everyone in the Lakewood club knew Eric Cahn. Never again would I have to cower before the Jaycees.

I immediately appointed my officers, and we formed a caravan of cars and headed west a half-mile to our favorite hangout, Lane's Tavern on West Colfax Avenue. The large neon sign proclaiming Lane's dwarfed the squat, square building with its painted, imitation log siding and its steeply pitched roof. The stream of cars easily crossed Colfax Avenue, practically devoid of traffic late on a weekday evening, and filed into the parking lot.

The sharp smell of cigarette smoke, mixed with the enticing odor of grilled meat, wafted out the door to greet us. We gathered into four vinyl-covered booths on the perimeter of the bar. We shouted to each other across the wooden tables, our voices raised out of exhilaration and necessity. We had to yell to prevail over the country western music booming from the jukebox.

It was almost too dim in the bar to read the menu, but I knew exactly what I wanted. I ordered my favorite, the famous Lane's hamburger, and a Seven Up. I had never enjoyed a meal so much. The sweet taste of victory mixed with the juicy meat, satiating me with a sense of happiness.

Often the Jaycees hung out at Lane's until 2:00 a.m. when it closed. But tonight I had other business.

I had written two letters to each of the men I had planned to appoint as officers, one in case of victory, the second in case of defeat. I happily tossed the defeat letters in the trash at Lane's. I left the tavern at 12:45 a.m. with the victory letters at my side and drove down the empty Colfax Avenue to the downtown post office. It was a fifteen-minute drive, and I enjoyed every minute of it. I smiled to myself as I dropped the notes in the mail slot. My new board members would receive the congratulatory notes the very next day.

Now came the hard work. First, I had to win over the members who had supported my opponent, Marlin Fisher. And we had another problem. Former chapter President Seary Nicoli was running for state president, and some in our chapter didn't support him. In fact, Seary barely squeaked out an endorsement from our chapter. That added to the disunity, and attendance was way down at our meetings.

As chapter president, it was my role to do everything possible to ensure Seary's victory. The election was to be held at the state convention, and Neva and I got there early to help with the campaign. We visited with members from throughout the state urging them to vote for Seary.

Our efforts paid off, and by the end of the convention, Seary was state president. But my troubles were not over. I was in the process of leaving my job at the Home, the Jaycee membership was split, and I was a wreck. My days were filled with trying to keep peace among the membership and put an end to the constant bickering and backbiting. I began to wonder why I had wanted this presidency, and one night I threatened to quit.

My supporters convinced me to stay. They promised that the bickering would soon be forgotten now that Seary was state president. So I went to the task with renewed vigor. The Jaycees became my second job, and I spent many hours each day on Jaycees work, whether writing letters, meeting with members or organizing activities.

A turning point came that summer. We had worked our tails off all spring on fund-raisers, community service projects and training for members. About twenty of us decided to attend the summer conference held at Adams State College in Alamosa, located in the center of the breath-taking San Luis Valley in south central Colorado.

The highlight of the conference was the Sunday afternoon lunch, attended by some 600 members from throughout Colorado, where the awards for the quarter were presented. The Lakewood members were sitting together when the surprise announcement came.

"Now it's time to announce the number one chapter of the quarter," said State President Seary Nicoli. "I am proud to announce it is my home chapter of Lakewood."

In stunned wonder and to a burst of applause and hurrahs from our membership, I strode proudly to the podium to accept the award. Lakewood had never been number one before, and the victory was particularly sweet in light of all we had suffered together.

As soon as we got back to Denver, the members who had been at the state conference got on the phone to the others. The message that we were "number one" passed quickly through the phone lines of Lakewood. Instantly our membership was reunited, and we went on to have a banner year. We were again named top chapter at the fall meeting, and the members were on top of the world.

Suddenly I was a hero in Lakewood, and the members wanted me to run for state office when I finished my year as local president. I agreed, and without opposition I was elected internal vice president of the Colorado Jaycees in 1969.

I had joined Great West Life as an insurance agent in May 1969 after a brief and disappointing stint at the Jewish Community Center. Working in insurance sales was never very lucrative for me, but it gave me the flexibility to spend most of my time doing Jaycees work.

I traveled around the state of Colorado, speaking to local chapters and encouraging them with special projects and membership drives. I was always willing to visit when a chapter needed help, and I drove hundreds of miles across snow-covered mountain passes to make a brief appearance at chapter meetings. I gained a lot of visibility around the state, and I was urged to run for state president.

In February 1970, I made the decision to try for the top spot in Colorado. I kicked off my campaign at my home chapter in Lakewood, and on February 24, the Board of Directors unanimously endorsed my campaign. A week later, the board presented my nomination to the Lakewood membership, and I received not only their support, but also a standing ovation. It was one of my finest moments as a Jaycee.

Although I was unopposed, I ran the campaign as if I had a tough competitor. I criss-crossed the state, from the old mountain mining town of Leadville to the eastern plains town of Burlington, just ten miles from the Kansas border. I came away with delegate pledges as I promised to continue to be a visible force in the state.

I was elected state president on May 21 at our state convention at the Ramada Inn in Greeley. I rose to the cheers of hundreds of fellow Jaycees and gave my first convention speech. Three days later, I drove home alone the fifty-four miles from the college town of Greeley to our house in Lakewood. I traveled southwest down the highway, breaking into a cold sweat. Could I really handle the responsibilities of the presidency? We had eighty-one chapters with 3,900 members now depending on me for leadership. What had I gotten myself into?

The first thing I did was organize an executive committee retreat. John King donated the use of his opulent ranch, located between the mountain resort towns of Winter Park and Granby, for the weekend. The rich food and plush accommodations fed my spirit, and I was ready to take on the challenges that were ahead.

I attacked the Jaycees' presidency with the tenacity of a man out to save the world. My income as an insurance salesman suffered as I made the Jaycees my primary job.

Behind the wheel of a donated Oldsmobile, I crossed Colorado as frequently as an interstate truck driver. Many of my trips were all-day affairs. I spent an abbreviated morning at my insurance work, then put on my Jaycee uniform, a leather bolero with "Lakewood" embroidered in red letters on the back, and headed down the long, dull road to Pueblo, or over twisting mountain passes to the Western Slope towns of Durango or Gunnison.

Eric as president of the Colorado Jaycees, 1970.

I arrived in the small towns across Colorado just in time for the evening meetings. I listened with interest to the chapter reports as I waited my turn to give an inspirational message. My trademark became the Irish blessing, with which I ended each speech. The blessing states, "May the road rise up to meet you. May the wind be always at your back. May the sun shine warm upon your face and the rains fall soft upon your fields... And until we meet again, may God hold you in the palm of his hand."

After firing up the troops and helping them plan special events, I got back in the Oldsmobile to head back to Denver. I generally refused offers to spend the night since I was most comfortable at home in my own bed.

Many times I felt myself beginning to doze as I roamed the deserted highways of Colorado and the clock ticked toward a new day. When I could no longer keep my eyes open, I pulled off on the side of the road and took a cat nap. I set off, renewed, for the last miles to Lakewood.

About midway through my year as president, General Motors had a strike, and the company asked me to return the loaned Oldsmobile. I replaced it with a red Volkswagen bug. One night as I headed back home, chugging up the 11,000-foot, snow-covered Monarch Pass, the mouse-breath heat in the Volkswagen gave out altogether. I shook and shivered as I topped the pass and headed down the eastern side of the Continental Divide. Visions of my nice warm bed kept me going.

Another night I was driving home from the mountains when I came upon a car with a boat hitched on the back. The boat had fish-tailed, and the car had gone off in a ditch on the side of the road. I stopped to help and got home at 4:00 a.m.

Sometimes I was so tired that I lost my sense of direction, and once I almost wound up in Kansas before I realized I was heading east when I needed to go west.

Vice President of the U.S. Jaycees Frank Antalek came to town in the middle of winter, and we did a two-day barnstorm of the state. Saturday afternoon we headed eighty-six miles east on Interstate 70 toward Limon, a farming community of 2,000 residents surrounded by endless miles of prairie. We drove past the town motels, a couple of grain elevators and a gas station, stopping at the cafe where the local chapter met. After a brief presentation, we got back in the Volkswagen and drove the eighty-six miles back to Lakewood. It was midnight when we stopped at my house. We stayed just long enough to change into fresh clothes.

Then it was back in the car. Destination: Craig, Colorado, a small farming and mining community 208 miles from Denver on the Western Slope. Craig was one of those Colorado town's where the elevation, 6,125 feet, exceeded the population. Craig, famous for its cattle and sheep, had begun to boom thanks to nearby oil, gas and coal exploration.

It was snowing heavily as we headed up Highway 40, and I arched my back and pushed my face toward the windshield. My knuckles turned white as I tightened my grip on the steering wheel. Frank and I bantered about the Jaycees, the light-hearted conversation masking my struggle against exhaustion and anxiety. The wind whipped the snow horizontally across the road, and my eyes strained to see the center line as we inched up the 11,000-foot Berthoud Pass. My foot rode the brake pedal as we came down the other side of the mountain, and I battled to retain control on the steep, icy descent.

The snow continued to fall steadily as we crept westward on the deserted road. It seemed to take hours to reach the summit of the 9,000-foot Rabbit Ears Pass and drop into Steamboat Springs. The roads were forsaken, and the Volkswagen made fresh tracks in the newly fallen snow. Darkness gave way to daylight when we finally straggled into Craig and headed into the VFW Hall for the Jaycees meeting.

The glamorous part of being state president was meeting with Governor John Love. Twice I was invited to the State Capitol to have my picture taken with him as he signed a proclamation honoring the Jaycees.

One proclamation was to recognize Honey Sunday, one of the highlights of my presidency. One of my fellow Lakewood chapter members had a retarded son, and we decided to have a fund-raiser for the Association for Retarded Citizens. It involved selling jars of honey across the state one Sunday in February.

We spent countless hours on the logistics of getting honey to every remote Jaycees community in Colorado. A wholesaler agreed to sell us the honey on consignment, and we had the jars delivered to all eighty-one Jaycees chapters. A publicity team organized a media blitz, and we had radio, television and newspaper coverage.

Eric met with Colorado Governor John Love in 1970 to sign a proclamation honoring the Jaycees.

When Honey Sunday arrived, our troops were mobilized — our 3,900 members were out in force. Some went door-to-door in their communities while others set up booths in shopping malls. Our Lakewood chapter placed stands at Westland and Villa Italia malls. Every citizen in Colorado had the chance to buy honey that day.

Each chapter called in their sales to the two co-chairs, Cliff Dodge and John McNutt. When all chapters had reported, the two men were so excited that they rushed over to my home.

"Eric, we sold 70,000 jars of honey!" Cliff cheered as I invited him in. "That means we've netted over $50,000 for mental retardation."

In 1970, $50,000 was a small fortune, and we had raised it in one day! My chest burst with pride as Cliff, John and I reviewed the glory of the day. The program later won a third-place community service award at the national Jaycees convention.

The Jaycees' national headquarters was in Tulsa, and Neva and I took a couple of trips there for special meetings. One time I returned home with $7.25 in my pocket, and my parking bill at the airport was $7.75. I had to talk fast to convince the attendant to let me go, and I promised to mail the fifty cents I owed.

The year passed in a whirlwind of activity, and I felt I was really doing something worthwhile and touching lives. Our fund-raising efforts were successful, and our membership was energized. While my work in insurance sales was unfulfilling, the Jaycees had brought new meaning to my life. When I left office in May 1971, it was clear that I would continue to move up the Jaycees' ladder.

Neva and the Colorado Jaycees urged me on, and I decided to run for a national vice president's slot in the summer of 1971. There were thirteen candidates for ten spots, and people assured me it would be easy to win a seat.

"Just go visit the delegates, talk to members and you'll get elected," they said.

I felt completely outclassed as I walked around the enormous convention hall in Portland. The other national candidates were more social, outgoing and aware of Jaycee politics. Though I had risen to favor in the organization, it was my management

*Victorious in his bid for a national vice presidency, Eric was given a ride
on the shoulders of his supporters at the national
Jaycees convention in Portland, summer 1971.*

skills, not my social demeanor, that had brought success. But my
reputation in Colorado held me in good stead, and I handily
won the election.

I had come a long way from the agonizing Christmas party
in Seary Nicoli's basement and from the bleak basement in
France. From the shy, new member that no one had known, I
was now a vice president of the 300,000-member U.S. Jaycees.

Before we left the Portland convention, we had a lottery to
choose the states we would serve for the coming year. I had the
chance to choose New York in the first round, a state I really wanted
because I knew many of the members. However, behind-the-scenes
politics came into play, and I was pressured to leave New York for
another vice president. So my first round pick was Wisconsin. In the

*Eric as vice president of the U.S. Jaycees in 1972. Ed Sievers,
president of the Iowa chapter, flew Eric around in his prop plane,
sometimes landing by the beam of car headlights.*

second round I chose Iowa, and in the third, Oregon. I was the last
person to pick in the fourth round, so I had no choice but Alaska.
And finally I got my home state of Colorado.

I soon learned why no one else wanted Alaska. I arrived in
Nome during a February snowstorm and met with the chapter
there. When I went to the airport the next day, I watched forlornly as my only chance of departure flew over the city. There
was a blizzard, and the plane couldn't even attempt a landing.
Day after day, I took a taxi from my hotel to the airport, waiting
in vain for the weather to improve enough for a plane to be able
to touch down. I had never seen so much snow in my life. I was
able to make my escape after a week when the snow let up
enough for the plane to pick up the stranded travelers in Nome.

I also had an aerial adventure in Iowa. Ed Sievers, the state president, was part-owner of a single-engine plane, and he flew me around the state to meet with chapters in isolated farm towns. One night, we flew into Washington, Iowa, after dark. Because the runway in the town had no lights, the members of the local Jaycee chapter lined up with their car lights on, and we found the runway via car power.

My favorite state was Oregon, and I marveled at the lush greenery as the state president drove me around. I visited each of my states at least twice and wrote a monthly newsletter to state presidents. I still spent enough time in my home state of Colorado that President Phil Winslow awarded me with the Gold Key Award, reserved for the top officer of the state. Generally the president would give it to one of his assistants, and I was overwhelmed with gratitude when Phil gave it to me although I was a national officer.

I gave 110 percent to my vice presidency and by the end of the year, I was burned out. I knew I could never be national president.

Chapter Twelve

"Why Are You So Late?"

One of the perks of being Colorado Jaycee president was to go to the Junior Chamber International World Congress, where Jaycees from all over the world came together. The Colorado Jaycee Ettes raised funds to pay for the trip for the president and his wife.

In 1970 when I was president, the International Congress was scheduled for Dublin, Ireland. I realized it was as close as I would ever get to Germany, and I thought I should seize the chance to visit Vater and my birthplace.

I'd had no contact with Vater since the early '50s, but I was determined to find him. I wanted him to see what I had become, to share the story of my success as a leader. I yearned for him to know that the clumsy young boy that he had scorned had matured into a competent family man. I was determined to seek Vater's approval one last time.

Using my best detective skills, I set out to find Vater. In the summer of 1970, I wrote a letter to the German Consulate in Bonn, giving a summary of my situation and asking if the consulate could provide any clues to Vater's whereabouts. The consulate replied with customary German efficiency, sending me two possible addresses.

I immediately sat down at my desk and started drafting a letter. I dug deep into my memory banks and uncovered the long-buried German language. I struggled to find the right words to explain why I was coming to Germany and to share my success in the Jaycees. I noted the date in October I would come to visit. Since I didn't know our exact plans for the visit, I wasn't specific about the time I would arrive at his home. I was filled with nervous anticipation as I made two copies of the letter and sent them off to the two addresses that the German consulate had provided.

In a couple of weeks, one of the letters came back, marked "addressee unknown." Each day I awaited the mail, like the young boy in Pueblo twenty years earlier, anticipating in vain a letter from Vater. My first question to Neva when I returned home from work was, "Any mail from Germany today?" The response was always the same, "Nothing."

The second letter didn't come back, so I surmised that Vater must have received it. Although his response was silence, I decided to proceed with my plans of going to Germany to see him. I wanted to visit my childhood home of Leutesdorf anyway, and the address for Vater was in Andernach, just a short ferry trip across the Rhein.

Neva and I attended the four-day Congress in Ireland, a whirlwind of activity with thousands of Jaycee VIPS from around the world. Neva was in her glory while I cringed at having to attend endless social hours where small talk flowed like

Irish beer. I was much happier at the business meetings when I could attend to the tasks at hand and avoid idle gossip.

I was enthralled with the history of the city, and each morning I would marvel at the dignity of the stone churches and palatial mansions as we walked from our hotel to the conference center. Even the post office, which I frequented daily to mail postcards to my supporters back home, had the majesty of an aging empress.

I was determined to bring back all the good ideas I could gather to make Colorado Jaycees better, and I focused all my attention on the conference. My days were filled with the bustle of meetings, the seemingly endless social events and sightseeing around Dublin. Each evening, I fell into my hotel bed exhausted, not squandering a moment of thought on my next destination.

The conference ended after four frenetic days. It was only then that I fully grasped, with a mixture of fear and anticipation, that I was headed to my homeland and Vater.

We bid goodbye to the Jaycees we had met at our hotel for American delegates, set our bags in the trunk of a taxi and headed for the airport. Next stop: Cologne.

I worried about how I would get along in Germany without speaking the language fluently. For two decades I carefully had buried it along with my memories of the years with Vater. I had erased any vestiges of my heritage, my accent and my native tongue in my bid to become an all-American boy.

The plane trip seemed so brief that I hardly felt prepared when we landed in Cologne. Neva and I collected our bags and headed over to the Avis Rental Car agency. I approached the counter, and in perfect German, I handled all the minutia related to renting a car. Neva looked at me with shocked surprise as I prattled in German. I was as surprised as Neva. I had no idea that I could so easily pluck the spoken language from the hidden recesses of my mind.

Neva, armed with a map of the area, navigated as I drove directly from Cologne to Leutesdorf. We made the hour's trip in silence, each involved in our own thoughts. The German countryside flashed by, overwhelming me with feelings of nostalgia. All the emotions that I had carefully submerged for two decades were bubbling to the surface like a pot of boiling water when the heat is turned on high.

I wondered about Vater. Did I really have the right address? How would he respond to me and I to him? Could we have a real family relationship after all these years of estrangement?

My mind was so busy with thoughts of Vater that I was surprised at how fast we arrived in Leutesdorf. Just as German had tripped smoothly off my tongue, so did my sense of Leutesdorf lead me down the right roads. I drove directly to the house at Haupstrasse 50 without hesitation.

I slowed the car to a stop and pulled up across the street from the house. It was a cool, cloudy day, and the white stucco walls of my childhood home were a spot of brightness. While I remembered the house as a dull gray, it was now a glossy white. A coat of paint and new windows had made all the difference in the world, and the house took on a quaint European charm that had eluded it twenty years earlier.

I was eager to see how the interior had changed and what memories my old bedroom would evoke. Stepping nervously up to the door, I rang the bell. No response. I rang again. Neva and I waited patiently for several minutes, but no one was home.

We turned away from the front door, disappointed, and began the steep ascent up the hill behind the house. As we topped the hill, my heart jumped. There, as if time had stood still for nature, were the endless rows of grape vines. Harvest had not yet come, and the vines drooped with the burden of their nearly ripe load.

I squinted down the rows and caught a glimpse of the young Erich laughing with the workers as he filled barrel after barrel with the juicy green grapes. My mouth watered as I remembered the taste of the sweet juice trickling down my throat. My fingers felt sore as I recalled the hours of uncoupling fruit from vine. I had experienced the peak of my childhood happiness on the vineyard hills, and viewing them again filled me with pathos.

We trekked back down the hill and away from the times of glory. I fought off the memory of the nadir of my childhood, the dark wine cellar that was the final resting place for the green grapes. I struggled to keep thoughts of my night of imprisonment in the cellar buried as deep as the cellar itself.

We got back to the tree-lined streets and decided to wander through the town for a little while. The trees were filled with the yellow, orange and red leaves of fall, and the ground beneath us was a blanket of color. Leutesdorf had put on a show for us.

We walked past a short, gray-haired woman in her seventies. She stared into my blue eyes and said, "You are Erich Cahn, son of Julius. You used to live in that house," she added, pointing at my childhood home. "I remember you."

Her face was vaguely familiar, but I could not identify her. Was she a neighbor? The parent of a childhood friend? I was too embarrassed to ask, so I told her that I was just visiting for the afternoon.

She said she would join us as we strolled down the street. In rapid German, she fired off twenty years' worth of small-town gossip. She told us countless stories about my childhood playmates: "X" had moved to Cologne, "Y" to Andernach. "Z" now had three children.

I had only a vague memory of most of the names she mentioned until she got around to our housekeeper, Theresa, the wicked witch of my childhood. Theresa, the old woman said, had gone crazy and been committed to a mental institution. I reacted without emotion. I had not thought about Theresa in years, having buried her along with the rest of the bitter memories of Germany. Now, remembering her mood swings and her vile temper, I was not surprised that she had suffered a breakdown. It seemed like a fitting end for the cruel housekeeper.

We sauntered aimlessly through the neighborhood streets, then down to the path that meandered along the Rhein. We walked along the grassy parkway with the chatty old woman continuing her monologue. Her constant prattle, along with my attempts to translate for Neva, kept me too busy to think or experience much emotion.

The woman escorted us back to the car after about a half-hour of walking, and we bid her farewell. She sent regards to my sister, but her attitude toward Vater was cold. Although she said nothing against him, I got the distinct impression that he was no longer well-respected in Leutesdorf.

We drove to the dock and loaded our rental car on the ferry to Andernach. We parked the car, and Neva and I got out to stand along the railing. It was a quiet day along the Rhein, and only a few small boats kept us company on the river.

I crossed my arms over my chest to shelter myself from the water's chill. White waves broke alongside the ferry, disturbing the serenity of the river's flow. My years of inner peace, bought at the price of purposeful denial of Vater's cruelty, were also being disrupted.

The Rhein River had played a leading role in my young life. It was the Rhein where my parents secluded me as a baby to protect us from the terror of Kristallnacht. It was the Rhein, seen from a train window, that gave me courage to face my duties when I went to Koblenz for my travel papers to America. The Rhein provided a sense of peace as Suzanne and I traveled with Vater by train to Munich and a new life. Now the Rhein was bringing me face-to-face with my history.

I looked back and saw Leutesdorf fading, the buildings taking on the appearance of dollhouses. Ahead Andernach was growing ever larger. As the expanse between me and Leutesdorf widened, I thought about the distance between Vater and me. Every chug of the ferry brought me closer in geography, but would we be able to bridge the gap of twenty years of silence? As Andernach loomed nearer, so did my anxiety.

I needed to stall for time, and we found a good reason. We arrived in Andernach in late afternoon, and we were famished. Andernach was considerably larger than Leutesdorf and we had no trouble finding a small cafe. After a quick, nondescript meal, we were once again on our way. It was time to face Vater.

I don't know if it was my mixed feelings about seeing him, or the confusing layout of the Andernach streets, but I made several wrong turns. I was getting tired and frustrated, and I couldn't seem to find his address. Twice I stopped and asked for directions.

Finally, I drove down a street of two-story row houses. The stone buildings all looked the same, and I slowed the car and searched for Vater's address. There, in the middle of the block, was his house. I pulled up across the street and brought the car to a stop. Anxiety made my hands clammy as I locked my car door and went around to open the passenger door for Neva. Silently, we crossed the street.

It was already early evening. I hesitated at the door, overcome by the unmet hopes of an eight-year-old boy at a reunion twenty-four years earlier. I prayed silently that this meeting would be different. My years of craving for parental love were focused like a laser point on this moment in time. The intensity of my longing burned a hole in my heart that I hoped Vater would fill. I mustered every ounce of courage I possessed and pressed the buzzer over the apartment marked "Cahn."

The shutters of a second-story window banged open. Vater, with the scowl of a scolding schoolmaster, glared down at me with his icy blue eyes.

"Why are you so late?" he bellowed, his first words after two decades of silence. I looked away and said nothing. Vater said he would come down to let us in, and he slammed the shutters closed.

Filled with the sour taste of his disapproval and neglect, I turned on my heels. I would not be hurt again. I would rather leave right now than face his ire. But Neva would not let me go.

"We traveled all this way to see your father, and now you're going to visit him," she insisted. She grabbed me by the arm and forced me to wait.

Vater opened the door, and I was overwhelmed once again by his hugeness. He still towered over me, and I had to look up to meet his gaze.

I stammered an apology like a child late from school.

"We had trouble finding the apartment. The streets here are confusing," I muttered in German, looking into the steely eyes that showed no forgiveness.

My dream had been to meet Vater as an equal and show him all I had accomplished, to make him proud of what I had become. But with a few terse words of disapproval, he reduced me to the inept child that he had sent away so many years before. The empty hole created by a childhood without love yawned wider.

The visit was already ruined, but we continued to go through the motions. Formally, Vater shook my hand. Then we turned toward Neva.

"This is my wife, Neva," I told him.

He shook her hand and invited us in. We followed him up the flight of stairs to his apartment, and I marveled at his mane of snowy white hair. He looked exactly the same to me: a big brute of a man whose very presence made me feel like a pipsqueak.

His wife waited at the top of the stairs. A stocky woman with brown hair, she greeted us solemnly. She was dressed formally in a two-piece brown suit, and she epitomized the cold, somber German to me.

Vater and his wife escorted us into the living room, where we sat on a dark wooden bench on one side of a long table. Vater and his wife sat on the other side. I looked across at a wooden shelf on the wall, decorated sparsely with one photograph of them and a few knickknacks.

We told them we had already eaten, and they offered us some coffee.

We sipped our drinks and engaged in the discourse of strangers. Vater talked about the German economy and asked me about money in America. While I would have liked to talk to him about my mother and my history, Vater kept the conversation light and impersonal. His wife sat at his side, stolidly listening to every word, and it was impossible for me to ask about my mother. Neva, not knowing a word of German, sat uncharacteristically silent.

The situation was as uncomfortable as the living room where we sat. I tried to talk about my job and children, but it was useless. My only thought was how soon I could gracefully escape. Nothing had changed during the years of our separation. I felt stifled under his gaze; he was still the cold authority figure who gave orders instead of love.

After a couple of hours of meaningless chatter, Neva and I rose to leave. The streets of Andernach were as dark as my spirits as Vater opened the door for us. He bid us "Auf Wiedersehen" without a kiss, a hug or a promise of future meetings.

Neva and I crossed the street. I helped her into the car, then quickly got in the driver's seat and revved the engine. I couldn't wait to put distance between Vater and myself.

Both Neva and I were suffering from severe headaches, so we drove in silence to Koblenz, where we had rented a room for the night. I slept fitfully under the crush of awakened emotions. I was eager for daybreak when I could put thousands of miles between me, Germany and my experience with Vater. We awoke early the next morning and drove directly to the airport. We flew to Paris, then back home to Colorado.

I never heard from Vater again. I learned years later that he died in December 1975.

Chapter Thirteen

A Matter of Ethics

During my year as national vice president of the Jaycees, I realized I had gone as high as I wanted to go. I had no desire to be the president of a 300,000-member organization despite my rewarding climb to power thus far. I knew I could handle the organizational side, but I was unprepared for the level of visibility that the national president endured.

I shuddered to think of working regularly with the national media or attending countless social events where I would have to make small talk. The shy little boy inside me shouted "no" when I even considered the idea for a moment.

At the same time, I was sorry to see my long, fulfilling involvement with the Jaycees come to an end. The Jaycees had become a shining spot not only in my life, but also in Neva's. I felt a real sense of loss as the year as national vice president wound down.

And then, what appeared to be the perfect solution fell into my arms like a gift from heaven. Just as my term was coming to an end, the paid position of executive vice president of the national Jaycees became available. Executive vice president was the top staff position, requiring behind-the-scenes organizational work rather than standing in the national spotlight. It was an opportunity to continue my love affair with the Jaycees without the pressures of the presidency. The job fit me like a well-tailored suit, and I was eager to go after it.

I had not been happy in my career since I left the Home in 1968. After quitting my job at the Home, I worked at the Jewish Community Center for a few, uncomfortable months. I was bored at the JCC because it didn't offer the same challenges and level of responsibility I had enjoyed at the Home.

Then there was the matter of religion. While the Home had a Jewish heritage, it was ecumenical because of the diverse religions represented by its residents. The JCC was heavily focused on Jewish programs and education. It was difficult for me to plan religious programs that no longer had meaning in my life. I had shed the overcoat of Judaism's rites and rituals when I first left the Home to go off to college. Like many college students, I had seized the freedom of college years to relinquish my past and explore new ideas. I came to realize that religion for me was a souvenir of sorrow. My memories of Judaism were tinged with pain. It was my religious heritage that caused me to lose my mother at the age of four. Then there were the painful memories of studying for my bar mitzvah with Opa. I could still recall the terrible fear of failure that accompanied those studies. So leaving Judaism was a relief from forgotten anguish.

My religious beliefs continued to fade as the years passed. By the time I married Neva, a Christian, I had no interest in religion.

Neva thought it was important for our children to learn the Jewish traditions, and she encouraged me to recapture the customs with them. Each winter we dusted off the menorah, the special candelabra for Chanukah, the Jewish Festival of Lights. I lit the candles with Jeff and Patti and told them the story of the Maccabees who recaptured the Jewish temple and relit the eternal flame. But my heart wasn't in it, and year after year, Neva had to prod me to go out and buy the special Chanukah candles. Finally she realized she was forcing the tradition on me, and she stopped. Without her reminders, I easily slipped out of the custom. By the time I went to work at JCC, neither Judaism nor any other religion played a role in my life.

So my few months at JCC were filled with inner conflict, and I was eager to move on. In May 1969, one of my Jaycees buddies encouraged me to join him in insurance sales.

I jumped at the chance to leave the stifling atmosphere of the JCC and work independently. Being an insurance salesman for Great West Life allowed me to be my own boss for the first time, and I relished that thought. I had grown tired of company politics and putting up with the whims of bosses. And with my growing involvement in Jaycees, I needed more flexibility in my schedule.

I loved the freedom of insurance sales, but I dreaded the work. My introverted personality stifled my success. Making cold calls was like walking into a crowded party filled with strangers. I struggled with the small talk and fought the urge to go hide in a corner. I felt a knot growing in my stomach every time I approached someone to make my sales pitch. Eventually that knot developed into an ulcer.

Working at the Home had filled me with satisfaction because I was lifting others up. I now felt I was dragging people down. I didn't like making people look at the inevitable, yet dark side of their future, and it showed. My negative feelings spoke louder than my sales talk, and I didn't sell much insurance. It was a vicious cycle where fear of failure brought on the result I feared.

I used my Jaycee work as a buffer against the pain of insurance sales. Given the choice between making cold insurance calls or working on Jaycee business, I always picked the Jaycees. That meant I spent less time earning a living and more on volunteer work.

Neva and I had started our marriage on a strong financial footing, and now we struggled to make ends meet. Neva went back to work as a secretary to help pay our bills.

That was the picture of my work life in 1972 when the job as executive vice president of the U.S. Jaycees became available. No wonder I jumped at the chance!

I was well-known in the Jaycees' hierarchy. So when the paid position opened up, I immediately received a call from the national office urging me to apply. It took only seconds to make my decision: I would go for the job even though it meant relocating the family to Tulsa. Neva was one hundred percent behind me. The Jaycees meant as much to her as to me, and she was thrilled at the chance to stay in the national spotlight.

I filled out the application with great care, listing my years of service with the Jaycees. I knew that I understood the organization as well as any potential applicant. I was secure in the knowledge that I'd make the final cut.

The weeks passed slowly as headquarters sifted through the many applications from around the nation. Finally the fateful phone call came from Tulsa. Six finalists had been selected, and I was one of them. The next step was to travel to Tulsa for an interview. Although my competition included another national vice president and national staff members, an inner voice whispered that I would be chosen.

I went through the interviews with the conviction that I was the best man for the job, and my attitude served me well. Just a few weeks before the 1972 Jaycee national convention in Atlanta, I was offered the executive job. I accepted without hesitation.

I flew back to Tulsa to meet the staff and explore my duties. I found that the executive vice president was responsible for running the headquarters with a staff of about twenty-five people and a sizable budget. My job at the Home had prepared me well as an administrator, and I felt prepared to run this monumental organization. All that remained was the formality of being approved by the executive committee at the convention.

Meanwhile, back in Denver, Neva and I had lots to do before going off to the national convention in Atlanta. Our timeline was short because we were expected to relocate to Tulsa right after the conference. We planned to attend the conference, return to Denver only long enough to pack up, and move immediately to Tulsa.

I tendered my resignation at Great West Life, and Neva resigned from her job as a secretary. Tearfully, we put our dearly beloved home on the market. It was a good time to sell real estate in Denver, and we had an offer almost immediately. Our new life was about to begin.

Neva and I arrived in Atlanta with Jeff and Patti in tow. Neva's exhilaration matched mine as I began shouldering the duties of my new, prestigious position with the national Jaycees. I felt heady as I saw the stacks of brochures printed with my photo, naming me as executive vice president. The brochures would be distributed at the end of the conference, just as soon as the new executive committee formally approved my appointment.

I could hardly wait to begin my new job, and my first chance was a big one. I was asked to run the national elections. I stood on the raised podium of the vast convention hall, looking down over some 12,000 assembly delegates, and I became dizzy with my newfound power.

The floor below me rocked with energized, boisterous Jaycees in their boleros and funny hats. Each state delegation was seated in a specific section marked by placards with the state name. Signs extolling the virtues of the candidates and bobbing balloons filled the air below me with a quilt of color and confusion. The roar of the crowd was deafening as delegates showed their support for the candidates as they were introduced. No Republican nor Democratic national conventioneer could top the enthusiasm of this crowd.

Political deals pervaded the meeting. The presidency in 1972 was a hotly contested race, with four candidates vying for the top spot. It would take several rounds of balloting to determine a winner. I was charged with making order out of the chaos on the convention floor.

Delegates were buzzing through the voting hall, and the wheeling and dealing had reached new heights. Supporters of certain candidates approached state delegations and asked them to leave the room for a chat. I was stunned to see these delegates leave the assembly floor with a lobbyist to caucus, then change their votes when they returned to the room. Some promise had been made, a deal struck, and loyalties changed as easily as the funny hats.

My favorite candidate was Dick Hahn of Indiana, and I felt certain he would win. He was the most qualified and most popular candidate. When it came down to the final ballot, the state president of Indiana made an impassioned speech on Dick's behalf. The whole crowd got caught up in it, and the room rocked with the sounds of cheering delegates. Hahn's victory seemed assured.

But his opponents wouldn't let it happen. They played parliamentary dirty tricks, keeping the doors of the voting hall tightly closed. No state delegation was allowed to leave the room for a caucus. That meant no state could change its votes back to Dick Hahn. The delegates were locked into both the room and what they had promised in previous deal-making.

I could hardly believe my eyes as I looked down at the dev-ilish games on the convention floor. The clamor was deafening. Delegates rumbled with bewilderment, then realized they had been duped. The wickedness of deceit boiled up from the hell below, and I felt myself being sucked into an inferno.

I banged the gavel against the lectern once, twice, three times, struggling to regain control of the meeting. Finally, the tumult subsided, and I was able to call for the vote. One by one the states shouted out their presidential preference. It was soon clear that Dick Hahn did not have enough delegates. Sam Winer of West Virginia was declared the new president of the U.S. Jaycees.

I was disappointed, angry and upset about how the elec-tioneering had gone. I had never seen this black side of the members, and I fell from innocence on the podium that day. What I observed on the convention floor made me realize there were snakes hidden in the perfectly manicured lawn of Jaycee decency. Now I wondered at the ethics of the organization I had chosen to lead.

I returned to my room weary from the anguish the election had wrought in my heart. I tossed and turned in my hotel bed, exhausted but unable to sleep.

I made one of the most difficult decisions of my life alone in the middle of the night. I decided I couldn't work for the new president, and more importantly, I couldn't deal with the political dirty tricks I had witnessed. I wanted no part of an organization where men manipulated others like puppets on a string. I would not be executive vice president if this is how the Jaycees operated.

I woke Neva early the next morning to break the news.

"I made a decision during the night. I'm not taking the job as executive vice president. I don't like these dirty politics," I told her.

She stared at me in shocked surprise and in a quavering voice said, "How can you do this Eric? You made a commit-ment. We sold our house, quit our jobs. This is a prestigious job that you fought for."

"I've made my decision," I repeated calmly.

"Think about me and the children. Please reconsider," Neva begged.

I turned a deaf ear to her pleas. I would not allow Neva's wishes to overrule my decision. It was my job, and I had made my choice alone in the dark of night. Stubbornly, I refused to think any more about it. I instinctively knew that if I went ahead with the job, I would be miserable. It wasn't going to happen.

Neva felt betrayed. She had been my partner in Jaycee activities for all these years. She had stood by my side, encourag-ing me to run for state and national office. She had been active in Jaycee Ettes, winning state awards. She had even worked in the state office. Now I was making the decision to sever our ties with Jaycees without even consulting her.

Neva continued to plead with me as she began to dress.

"Please think this over. Don't rush into anything. You don't need to call anyone right away. Let's talk," Neva urged.

I wouldn't listen. I ignored her strong objections, picked up the hotel room phone and dialed the room of the newly elected president.

"I'm sorry," I said. "After witnessing the election yesterday, I've decided I can't serve as executive vice president. I'm refus-ing the position," I told a shocked Sam Winer. It took a moment for my message to sink in.

"Please don't make a hasty decision Eric. We really want you for this job. Please reconsider," he said.

But I would not be moved. If Neva couldn't change my mind, no one else would either.

The news of my dramatic resignation spread like wildfire as Sam tried to change my mind through friends. In a few minutes, the phone in our hotel room began to ring.

"Please reconsider Eric, look at this in perspective," the top brass of Jaycees pleaded. "The election is just one small part of our work. Think about all the good things you have done with the Jaycees over the years."

Even Dick Hahn, the defeated candidate, called to urge me to rethink my decision. The incessant phone calls only had the effect of making me more steadfast in my resolve. These men would not wear me down.

The convention had ended after the election, and it was time to head for home. Neva and I packed our bags in uneasy silence, broken only by the chronic jangling of the telephone. I focused all my energy on getting Neva and the kids away from the charged atmosphere of the convention center. I just wanted to be back home.

Neva and I sat in stony silence through the long flight back to Denver. She was furious that I had turned away this once-in-a-lifetime opportunity without even a moment's consultation. I knew she was angry and avoided her gaze.

Jeff and Patti could tell something was terribly wrong. They too sat quietly on the plane ride, not wanting to disturb their obviously distraught parents.

As I sat uncomfortably next to Neva on the plane, my mind vacillated from the past to the future — what I had just done and what I had to do back home. Though I had wrought havoc in the Jaycee organization, I was sure I had made the right choice. Now I had to face the uncertain future I had created.

The work waiting in Denver seemed monumental. I would have to untie all the tidy knots I had made in preparation for the move to Tulsa. I prayed that I could go my job back. And there was the matter of the house. Could we go back on our agreement to sell it? Could Neva get her old job back? I couldn't wait to get home and unravel the mess I had made.

The first person I called when I got home was Bob Perkins, my Great West manager. He was more than willing to take me back. Fortunately, none of my resignation paperwork had been sent to the home office. As far as Great West Life knew, I had never considered leaving. Knowing I still had my insurance job was like a security blanket as I faced the continued onslaught from the Jaycees.

And an onslaught it was. We were still unpacking our suit-cases when the cacophony of phone ringing resumed. Jaycee officers from around the nation took up where they had left off in Atlanta.

After a while, I avoided answering the phone because I knew it would be a repeat of the previous call. Repeating my stock answer, "No, I will not reconsider," was wearing me out. I just wanted to be left alone to get on with my old life.

I even dreaded answering the doorbell. Telegrams began arriving from across the country begging me to reconsider. Another man might have been flattered by the attention, but I was embarrassed and annoyed by it. My decision was made, and there was no turning back. Why wouldn't they leave me alone?

Unbeknownst to me, Neva continued to hope I would change my mind. She imagined that every ring of the phone would bring the magic call that would convince me of my error. Her own dreams pushed aside the reality of the situation, and she actually thought that I was reconsidering.

Neva bustled around the house, putting things in order. I watched with amazement when I realized she was still readying the family for the move to Tulsa. Finally I confronted her.

"You don't have to get anything ready, Neva. I told you that we're not going to Tulsa. I've made up my mind to stay here and I'm not changing it," I said in a tone that banned discussion.

She looked at me with the eyes of a wounded puppy. Slowly, it dawned on her that she had absolutely no influence on the most monumental decision of our lives. I was turning her world upside down, yet I would not take her wishes into account.

Neva went into a tailspin. She was agitated not only by my decision, but also by my attitude. The fact that I didn't consider her feelings in making the decision was more than she could bear. She felt broken and deceived.

The next morning, Neva left the house and went to visit her brother. She talked to him about what had happened but couldn't shed the despair she felt. After a few hours she left her brother's house without a destination. She aimlessly wandered the streets of Denver for hours, not wanting to come home and face me.

Finally, she wound up at the Ramada Foothills hotel where she spent the night. The next morning, distraught and confused, she went to the doctor. Seeing her fragile emotional state, he checked her into Bethesda Medical Center. She needed a place to recuperate from what had become a most traumatic experience in her life.

The doctor called me, and I brought a suitcase with some of Neva's clothes to the hospital. I too was in a state of shock. I was so wrapped up in my own needs that I hadn't realized the depth of Neva's emotional upheaval.

When I got home from the hospital, the kids were playing in the backyard. Patti was almost eleven, and Jeff, nine. I approached them cautiously.

"Your mother isn't feeling well, and she's going to be in the hospital for a few days," I said, choking back tears. I was trying to keep the emotion from my voice, but I couldn't control my anguish. Patti and Jeff had never seen me cry, and they were alarmed by what was happening. They acted nonchalant, playing along with my desire to hide my feelings. They avoided my eyes and turned back to their game of ball. I went inside the house to pull myself together.

I drifted aimlessly through the week, drowning in a sea of despair. I had survived the biggest career decision of my life and the almost unbearable pressure from the Jaycees that followed. Now I was faced with Neva's depression and my guilt. It was the darkest period in our lives together.

The small details of day-to-day life seemed overwhelming. I had the unfamiliar job of running the household as well as working. I had returned to my job in insurance sales, but my heart wasn't in it. I came home for lunch each day to straighten up the house and check on the kids. Then I returned to work for another long afternoon, forcing myself to concentrate on making a living.

I was mentally and physically exhausted when I arrived home early in the evening to fix dinner. We ate together silently, each wrapped up in our own thoughts. As kids, they were engrossed in their own activities. They asked few questions about what was happening between their mom and me, and I offered no explanations. I successfully hid the gravity of the situation from them.

Neva returned home after a week, and on the surface, life went back to normal. But it was a turning point not only in my career, but also in our marriage. I realized that the rift in our relationship could never be completely healed. I knew deep in my heart that some day our marriage would be over. I wanted the kids to grow up in an intact home, and I vowed to try and make the marriage work for now.

Neva was also coming to terms with our differences. Through counseling, she came to the conclusion that she couldn't influence my decisions as much as she would like. She would have to accept that I would make my own career choices without her counsel. Neva decided she could no longer live through my life. She would find her own way, and become an independent, successful person in her own right.

We peacefully co-existed, but a hole had been ripped in the fabric of our relationship, and nothing seemed to repair it. It was torn wider by the loss of the Jaycees in our social life. I had reached the end of my volunteer career and now had terminated any possibility of a professional position with the Jaycees. We were no longer involved in the activities that had become so much a part of our lives.

The only thing we seemed to have in common was our devotion to our children. I rededicated myself to Patti and Jeff, and the kids became my life. I lived through their successes. Patti had become quite a talented horsewoman and was bringing home ribbons in English riding. Watching her take the jumps with an air of self-assurance filled me with fatherly pride. I was grateful I was able to give her the simple pleasures of childhood that I had missed.

Jeff was in Little League football and practicing with him was one of my greatest joys. After work he and I walked over to the park to practice throwing, catching and doing wind sprints. I coached him with patience and pride as he developed into a skillful athlete. Our hours in the park brought back joyful memories of my cross-country days and the strenuous workouts that had carried me to triumph. In the ballpark with Jeff, I could forget about my troubled marriage and mediocre career, and revel in the joy of parenting.

Patti's and Jeff's activities filled the summer days, and we looked like a normal, happy American family at play. Our marital relationship, however, continued to deteriorate. Our fights became more frequent, and the words more angry. Although we tried to hide our differences from the kids, you could almost cut the tension in our home with a knife. A couple of times I threatened divorce.

Chapter Fourteen

End of an Era

Neva and I were like oil and water. While she was gregarious, fun-loving and spontaneous, I was shy, somber and pensive. Neva wanted to be surrounded by people; I preferred solitude.

Even our attitudes about housekeeping conflicted. Neva didn't follow the children around, wiping up after them, but I had to. I couldn't bear a speck of dust or a misplaced dish.

Like many Holocaust survivors, I demanded extreme tidiness in my home. Perhaps it is a lifelong need to overcome the wretchedness of the camps. The filthy stench of life under Nazi domination was enough squalor to last a lifetime; now we needed to be surrounded by cleanliness and serenity.

Even though I had no conscious memory of my family's miserable existence in Camp Gurs, it apparently left an indelible mark on me. What other people considered rustic, I saw as crude.

What others called "lived-in," I judged as sloppy. I longed for a spick-and-span, orderly home where not one dirty dish lingered in the sink.

I was unable to bear even a moment of disarray, so I took over some of the chores to find tranquility in my home. My insurance sales hours were flexible, and I generally came home for lunch. No one else was at home, and I couldn't enjoy my meal until I tidied up. I walked from room to room gathering laundry and loading it into the washer.

I approached the kitchen with trepidation. I stopped in the entryway, surveyed the scene and inventoried what my children had left behind that morning. Once again they had failed my test of cleanliness with a long list of transgressions — fingerprints up and down the refrigerator door; a sink brimming with unwashed breakfast dishes; and cereal boxes lining the kitchen table.

I grabbed the Windex bottle and a sponge and began spraying away the signs of my children's disregard for tidiness. I stacked the dishes in the dishwasher and hid the cereal behind the cupboard door.

I grabbed a yellow, lined legal pad from the desk drawer, and in a rare act of discipline, scrawled across the top sheet, "I am very ANGRY and disappointed. Please clean up after yourselves!!!!!" I left the note in the middle of the now-spotless dining room table and headed back to work.

My missives, however, were in vain. The children continued to leave the crumbs of indifference scattered throughout the house. Neva remained unruffled and unchanged by my compulsive need for absolute order.

Our housekeeping styles reflected how we approached life. While Neva sought freedom, I craved order. She was carefree; I tried to structure every detail of our lives. Neva gushed with emotion. I kept all my possessions — including my feelings — neatly tucked behind closed doors.

I was often quite moody, sinking into deep depressions, but I refused to look at the cause. I wasn't ready for self-exploration; I didn't have the strength to examine how the past continued to torture me. So the losses of my youth remained buried under decades of carefully developed defenses. When feelings of despair bubbled up, I squashed them back down. The effort exhausted and depressed me.

But I refused to ask for help, even from Neva. Instead I moped around the house. Neva and the kids instinctively knew when I was in a dark mood, and they tiptoed around me. They walked as if on eggshells, trying to avoid intensifying my pain through any household disruptions. It was a tranquility made of deception, but the only one I could bear.

Neva, on the other hand, wore her emotions on her sleeve. She was quick to laugh and just as quick to anger. Avoidance was my mode of relating, where confrontation was hers. I prevailed for the first decade of our relationship. We had few arguments, and the serenity I craved was maintained.

However, when I gave up the Jaycees job in Atlanta, our relationship was altered for all time. A Cold War ensued, and we co-existed in a fragile peace. Then Neva tried to prod me into discussion by chipping away at our differences. When I refused to open up, she resorted to screaming. Finally, I could bear it no longer, and I shouted back. Our home rocked in an earthquake of emotion. The number of skirmishes grew as the years progressed, and the cracks in our tranquility magnified into dangerous fissures.

Eventually shouting matches became our primary mode of communication. The fights grew more frequent and more violent. One day, Neva bent down, pulled the clogs off her feet, and hurled them across the room as I ducked for cover.

I craved a safe haven from the demands of the outside world, and my home was now a war zone. I approached the house with apprehension each night, wondering if I would make it through the evening in peace. The thought of divorce swept through my mind with increasing frequency.

Many of our arguments centered around Patti and Jeff. My childhood had been hell; I wanted paradise for my children. Reacting to my own deprived upbringing, I vowed my children would want for nothing. Not only did I shower them with affection, but I also catered to their every whim. I couldn't tolerate denying them any pleasure.

Neva became the Scrooge to my year-round Santa Claus. I was unable to criticize my children nor discipline them. That job fell solely on Neva's shoulders. She couldn't even depend on me to support her actions.

The kids quickly learned how to work us. When they asked Neva if they could do something and she said "no," they appealed to me. Time after time I relented. I didn't realize how I was isolating Neva and making her the bad guy in the family.

A volatile relationship between mother and daughter compounded the problem. Patti developed a temper like her mother's, and they shouted their way through Patti's rocky teenage years. They could hardly be in a room together without taunting each other, like picking a scab so the wound could never completely heal.

Neva could never win. Patti huffed out of the house if Neva was near victory.

"I'm running away from home," she shouted tearfully as she slammed the front door behind her.

I panicked. I had suffered too many losses in my childhood to endure the thought of losing my own child. I was terrified she'd get hurt as she raced away from the security of our home.

The door had barely slammed shut as I pulled it open again. I rushed down the street after her, summoning my cross-country racer's skills to catch up.

"Please, Patti. It will be all right. Don't do this to me. Please come home," I begged, grabbing her arm.

Pouting, she complained about how unfair her mother was.

I persisted, "Come home. Let me take care of it. I hate to see you unhappy."

Patti softened when she sensed my grief. As much as she wanted to punish her mother, she was incapable of hurting me. We walked hand in hand back to the house as Patti brushed the tears from her face.

Neva watched the predictable scene through the window, shaking her head in disgust. She had lost yet another round in the battle to discipline our children. I took Patti's side over Neva's, whatever the issue, eroding both her control over the children and our marriage.

One of the few joys we shared in those years was a love of our home. Our house on Applewood Knolls Drive was a beautiful ranch in a neighborhood surrounded by the protective shrubbery of upwardly mobile, middle-class families. On the surface, we were like all the other families on the typically suburban block, over-indulging our children in our quest to grab hold of the American dream.

But as my business faltered, it became increasingly difficult to keep our arms around the dream. Our neighbors were professionals — bank presidents, doctors and lawyers — who were climbing the ladder to success. Their children had all the latest fashions and participated in all the trendy, expensive activities. We tried to give our children the same advantages. Patti had joined the neighbor girls in an English horseback-riding club, but the cost became more than our family budget could withstand.

Something had to change in 1975, four years after the Atlanta fiasco where I refused the Jaycees job. Neva and I decided we had to relinquish our beloved home and move into a neighborhood where the people were on our step of the economic ladder.

Change was always difficult for me, but this was devastating. Not only was I giving up my dream home, but I also had to admit defeat as a breadwinner. I could no longer support my family in the manner to which we had grown accustomed. We were taking a giant step backward, and it was my fault. My ego suffered a terrible blow as I packed our belongings. Although the new house was a few short blocks from the old, it was miles away in terms of prestige and elegance.

The small, dark house on Quail Street never felt like home. It was a grim house that Patti said had "bad karma." The kids on the block did nothing to allay our feelings of despair about the new house. The neighborhood rascals, quick to spread rumors about the previous owners, put fear into Patti's and Jeff's hearts.

"The people who lived there before always kept their curtains drawn. They did terrible things in there. They even locked their little boy in the bedroom," the young residents revealed.

It didn't matter how much truth the story held. It sealed our feelings about the house as a dismal place. We did our best to spruce up the yard, planting flowers and manicuring the neglected lawn. Neva took the house on as a challenge and devoted her ceaseless energy to making it more comfortable and homey. She painted and decorated, adding colorful touches to chip away at the bleakness of the house. But no matter what we did inside or out, our hearts were heavy as long as we lived there. We all continued to pine for the Applewood Knolls place and the years of prosperity it represented.

Luckily, we only had to endure the grim little place for three years. I got involved in some real estate deals in addition to my insurance sales, and our financial fortunes took a turn for the better. The first thing we decided to do with our newfound money was move to a nicer home.

It was 1978 when we moved to a brand-new house. A bright, clean place, the house improved everyone's attitude. I was pleased that I had provided a better home for my family, and my ego recovered from the blow it had suffered when we left our upscale home on Applewood Knolls Drive. The kids were happy to be out of the small, dark house on Quail Street. And Neva was in her glory. It gave her the chance to decorate a house from scratch and landscape the yard her way. This time, she didn't have to fix someone else's decorating errors. She could have things exactly as she wanted them.

Neva was also enjoying her work life more than ever before. She had gotten a job at Lutheran Hospital in Wheat Ridge, not far from our home. Lutheran was the only hospital in Jefferson County, a rapidly growing gaggle of towns, cities and communities, including Lakewood and Wheat Ridge. Immediately to the east was Denver. The hospital, originally built for tuberculosis patients, was now a community health care center, growing as rapidly as the suburbs.

Neva's gregarious nature held her in good stead at the hospital, and she was quickly promoted. She kept earning raises, increasing her salary by twenty-two percent in the first two years. When the hospital created the position of patient representative, Neva was chosen for the post. It was a perfect fit for the outgoing, people-loving Neva. She was finally finding an outlet for her creative energies.

Unfortunately, life at home continued to deteriorate. Changing houses and jobs did nothing to quiet the wars on the home front. Our marital skirmishes grew more frequent and severe.

The challenges of raising the children intensified as they grew up. When Patti became a teen-ager, she and Neva got into a battle of the wills with increasing frequency. The pattern I had established in Patti's preteen years continued. Neva and Patti would argue, and I would take Patti's side, infuriating Neva more with each fight.

It was inevitable that the issue would finally come to a head. The only question was when it would happen and what would precipitate it.

The blowup came just prior to Patti's high school graduation in May 1980. Patti came home from school, and Neva was already at home. Neva had been listening to her favorite music on the stereo. Without a word of greeting, Patti went over to the stereo and flicked the switch. She wanted to listen to rock'n'roll.

Neva was furious. It was the final skirmish in a constant battle for control. Neva began shouting.

"I was listening to my music. Don't you have any respect for me? How can you come in here and change the station as if I don't exist?"

Patti fought back, her temper flaring. The battle raged on, with voices and emotions escalating. In the heat of the fight, both tried to do injury with all the emotional weaponry they could muster.

Finally, Patti yelled, "I don't want you to come to my graduation. I want Dad to come, but you can stay home."

Those words out of Patti's mouth, mother and daughter recoiled in fury. The two of them, spent of energy and anger, moved as far apart as the house would allow.

I sensed danger as soon as I opened the front door. The air in the house was heavy with the weight of their anger. I was scorched by the heat of intense emotions, and I wanted to cool things down right away. I approached Patti and Neva and asked what had happened.

Each woman privately told me her emotion-laden version of the story, and a gaping hole grew in the pit of my stomach. I felt the fragile peace of our home shatter into thousands of pieces. I instinctively knew that things had gone too far this time. But I had to give peacemaking a try.

"Please, Neva," I begged. "Please come to Patti's graduation. It's a once-in-a-lifetime event, and you'll be sorry you missed it later."

But Neva refused to relent.

"She doesn't want me there, and I'm not going," Neva said with stubborn finality.

Patti, too, declined to surrender. She would neither ask for forgiveness nor invite her mother to the graduation. The toxic words had been spoken, and they couldn't be unsaid. The air between them was poisoned. As hard as I tried, I couldn't find the antidote.

I continued to cajole Patti and Neva until the very last moment. When the day of graduation arrived, I beseeched Neva one last time to reconsider. I was sure she would change her mind. I couldn't fathom how she could miss this most special day in our lives. But Neva refused to attend. She stayed resolutely in the bedroom when Patti and I went off to the ceremonies at Wheat Ridge High.

I climbed into the stadium risers in a state of shock. How could we have fallen so far as a family? How could this day, a glorious occasion, turn into such a disaster?

I took a seat, a solitary figure surrounded by tight-knit circles of proud families. I yearned to be a proud father, with my loved ones encircling me, basking in the warmth of my daughter's success. But I was alone.

The roll of graduates was called, and I watched with tears in my eyes as my only daughter, my firstborn, shook hands with the principal and received her diploma. I was transported back in time to my own graduation day, twenty-four years before. A cold chill ran down my spine, and I trembled. It dawned on me that nothing had changed in all those years. I had been despondent with loneliness at my own graduation, and I was just as forlorn now.

The speeches droned on, but I stopped hearing the words. I began to reflect on my life. What good was my marriage if we couldn't share these moments? What kind of relationship did we have if I couldn't even convince Neva to come with me on this important day? Was it time to stop deceiving myself and realize that my marriage was never going to get any better? Was it worth hanging around "for the kids?"

I reached a decision while I was sitting there, isolated from the crowd. I too would experience a commencement in my life. The time had come to divorce Neva. I had waited long enough.

When the fanfare was over, Patti and I found each other through the throngs and headed back to the car. We were both quietly reflective, Patti thinking about her future in college and I pondering a future without Neva. Patti didn't notice the change in me, but I felt like a new person.

Patti and I quietly entered the house. Neva stayed hidden in the bedroom while Patti quickly changed her clothes and set off for the traditional round of parties. She was eager to celebrate with her friends.

Jeff was away from home too, and I decided I might as well act immediately. I confronted Neva as soon as Patti left.

"This is it. I can't live like this any more," I stated flatly.

Before Neva could say a word of disagreement or ask a question, I went on.

"I want a divorce, and I want us to separate immediately. Do you want me to leave this house, or are you leaving?" I demanded.

Neva looked at me in shocked surprise. She was unaccustomed to this kind of confrontation from me. Generally, she was the one who started the discussions. I had always avoided arguments; now I was being the aggressor. Instinctively, she knew that this was a turning point in our lives.

She lashed out at me. "You take the house and the kids. I'm leaving," Neva shouted.

She turned from the room without another word. She pulled a few things from the closet and stormed out the door.

It was the end of an era.

Chapter Fifteen

Another Chance

I slipped into bachelorhood with a mixture of trepidation and excitement, like a man buying his first new pair of shoes in many years. Although the old pair was tattered and no longer fit, there was comfort in its familiarity. But the thrill of a brand-new, better-fitting pair helped me walk forward into a new stage of life.

Patti was thrilled to be freed from the constant tension with her mother, but Jeff missed Neva terribly. We struggled through the summer as I learned to be a single parent, cooking and taking care of the house.

Neva and I started seeing each other after the original shock of our separation subsided. I called her regularly at her aunt's house to see how she was doing. She came over to visit the kids and to help me learn how to cook.

We developed a pattern of early morning meetings at Sloan's Lake Park, the park that had played such a central role in my life. Sloan's Lake was where I had learned to drive, and it was where I ran to escape the pain of losing Doris. Now I was returning to the lake to soften the blow of my separation from Neva. We sat in my 1978 gray and black Mercury Cougar in the parking lot overlooking the lake and talked about the kids until it was time to leave for work. We clung to the fragile thread of our past relationship to help us make the transition to the future. Neva hinted at reconciliation, but I had closed and locked the door behind me.

Our divorce was final by October. I had begun dating other women, and I was enjoying my newfound freedom. Then a strange thing happened. I began to see Neva in a different light. Freed from the shackles of our day-to-day arguments, I remembered what had attracted me to Neva two decades earlier. Her bubbly personality won me over once again, and we began to date. I enjoyed being with her, and we even took country swing dance lessons.

Patti and Jeff were totally confused. They had come to accept the divorce, and now there appeared to be a chance that we'd get back together. The kids didn't know what to think, and neither did we. It didn't seem healthy, yet I was unable to let go. She was still my security blanket, and I didn't have the strength to move forward without her. I continued dating Neva and occasionally other women for two years. Then I met Jane.

Neva was still working at Lutheran Hospital, and she asked me to go with her to the Christmas dance. As Neva and I were dancing, I noticed a group of people across the room. I was smitten by an attractive redhead in a bright green dress. She and two other women were frolicking with the president of the hospital, Jim Willard. The woman looked so alive, filled with vivacity, that I couldn't take my eyes off her. I admired her from afar for the rest of the evening.

The next day, Neva and I went downtown Denver to shop for Christmas presents for the kids. We entered a ski shop in Larimer Square, an old area of downtown Denver revitalized with fashionable boutiques and trendy restaurants. The street was decked out in its Christmas finery, and holiday spirit filled the air. I looked into the shop, and magically, the "woman in the green dress" was inside. I recognized her immediately from the night before and once again was attracted to her vitality.

Neva spotted her as well.

"Eric, I'd like you to meet Jane, a social worker at the hospital," Neva said.

"Pleased to meet you," I said. We shook hands, and I tingled from her touch.

We continued to talk for a few minutes, recounting the dance of the night before. I blurted out what I was thinking with the naive honesty of a child.

"I enjoyed watching you dance last night, Jane," I said.

Neva and Jane both looked at me with surprise, but neither they, nor Jane's friend, Dixie Davis, responded. After a few more minutes of chatting, Neva and I went our way, and they went theirs.

Meanwhile, things with Neva were coming to a head. The kids and I were at Neva's house for Christmas Eve, and we were talking about spending the night there for the first time. Outside, a blizzard was quickly covering the streets with a treacherous layer of ice.

The phone rang, and it was a colleague from Lutheran Hospital. I couldn't hear what the caller asked, but Neva replied, "I understand. Sure, I'll be right there."

She placed the phone back on the receiver and told us she was going to hospital. The caller had asked Neva to help out because she had a four-wheel drive car and lived nearby. She could get through the storm to the hospital; a lot of others couldn't. I was furious that she put her job before the family. She hadn't even hesitated, or consulted us, before making her decision to leave.

I knew at that moment that getting back together was impossible. I could never accept taking the backseat to her career.

I was at Lutheran Hospital on business a few days later, and I passed Jane in the hall. We acknowledged each other with a "hi" and continued in opposite directions. I turned around, wanting to catch another glimpse of her. She turned at the same moment, and we exchanged bashful smiles.

That was all the encouragement I needed to ask Jane on a date. Her office mate was a friend of Neva's, and I brazenly asked the woman to get me Jane's phone number. I immediately called and asked Jane to lunch.

I drove up to Jane's door in east Denver at noon Saturday, January 29, 1983, in my Mercury Cougar. I had been dating for awhile, but this time I felt more nervous than usual. Jane came to the door and smiled radiantly at me.

Her ex-brother-in-law was installing some closets for her, and she told him she was leaving as she came out the door to meet me. I held the door of the Cougar opened for her as she gracefully held her skirt and got into the car. I had decided to take her back across town to Jonathan's, one of the premier restaurants in Lakewood and my favorite hangout. I needed the comfort of an old haunt to help me through the anxiety of a first date.

The awkwardness between us melted away in moments. As was my habit, I began by asking her about herself. It was my way of hiding behind my questions. Jane was the most open person I had ever dated. She revealed not only her experiences, but also her sentiments about her southern Baptist upbringing in Tulsa, her career as a social worker, and her failed first marriage.

Then Jane smiled at me and asked about my background. Suddenly, I was opening my heart in a way I had never done before. I told Jane all about my childhood in Germany and moving to America to live with Oma and Opa. I shared my experiences with the Jaycees, and my visits to Tulsa, her hometown.

Our backgrounds were as different as night and day, yet there was an undeniable magnetism between us. Our first date turned into a four-hour marathon, and our patient waiter allowed us to sit in the restaurant long after the lunch crowd had come and gone.

Finally, Jane said she had to get back home and see how her brother-in-law was doing with the closets. I dropped her off at home, then drove back across town in a daze. My heart was stirring with feelings that I had not encountered since I was a high school boy in the throes of my first love. I yearned to spend more time with this wonderful woman.

I resisted calling Jane the following day, but she was constantly on my mind. By the time Monday came, I was a man obsessed. I could wait no longer to hear her voice. I had just found out that I passed the certified financial planner exam, and I wanted to share the news with her. I asked her to meet me for a drink to celebrate.

Jane met me at the Jefferson 440 restaurant, an elegant eatery where soft lighting and cushioned booths provided an atmosphere of intimacy. We settled into a booth, and I ordered a Seven Up, and Jane had a glass of white wine. I could hardly take my eyes off her as I sipped my soda. We chatted as if we had known each other for years. The minutes passed too quickly, and it was time for me to leave. I had to get back to the office by 7:30 to meet a client. I offered to walk her to her car and couldn't hide my surprise when she stopped at a sporty orange and white Porsche.

"This is your car?" I asked with a quizzical look on my face.

As she turned to answer, I kissed her for the first time. It was instant captivation. I drove back to the office in a trance, and I could hardly concentrate on my client's finances. I just wanted to be with Jane again.

I stumbled my way through the appointment and with relief, escorted the client to the door. Then I rushed back into the office and dialed Jane's number.

"Our kiss was so wonderful that I feel ten feet tall and ten feet off the ground," I gushed as soon as she answered.

She listened quietly as I spilled my heart. I didn't know it then, but she too was overcome with feelings. From that day forth, we were totally, passionately devoted to each other. Neither one of us had room for anyone else in our lives.

Even when I was with others, I was biding my time to be with Jane. I played volleyball once a week with my old friend Chuck Toft from the Home, and we finished at 10:30 p.m. I called Jane and asked if I could stop by after the game. I was in heaven when she said yes. Sometimes she would meet me in a little bar on the east side of town. She sipped a glass of white wine as I stared into her brown eyes with love.

The magnetism between us was so strong that we reacted totally from the heart, not giving our heads the chance to issue any warnings to slow down. We were practically living together after only two weeks.

Each night after work, I'd race to Jane's house on Forest Street. But I didn't move in; none of my personal possessions were at her house. Instead, I woke up at 5:00 a.m. and headed back to my house in Lakewood. There I'd feed our dog, Tramp, a shaggy, black poodle mix, and get ready for work.

Jane brought out the romantic in me. On Valentine's Day, I sent her a dozen long-stemmed red roses. That night, she was hosting a dinner party for a group of single women friends. All of them were in the midst of a crisis in their relationships or had just broken up with their boyfriends. Jane didn't want to flaunt her new relationship, so she hid the roses in her bedroom.

Jane fidgeted and fiddled all night. She just couldn't keep her new relationship a secret. So she told her friends about the depth of our feelings for each other, and the roses came out of the bedroom with a flourish.

Our relationship was permanently cemented the night we went to see the movie "Sophie's Choice." The scenes of Nazi Germany tore at my heart, and I drew strength from Jane sitting beside me. I realized how well she understood and nurtured me. The bond between us was growing stronger every day.

In March we decided to take our first trip together to celebrate my birthday. We planned to go to Colorado Springs, seventy miles south of Denver, and stay in the elegant Four Seasons Hotel. Unfortunately, one of Colorado's famous spring blizzards hit, and the interstate was a muddle of slush and sliding cars. It took us hours to make our way tediously down the slick highway. But Jane was at my side, and that was all that mattered.

The weather was so awful that we were confined to the hotel all weekend, but that didn't matter either. We basked in each other's company, enjoyed leisurely meals, and had plenty of time to talk. It was inevitable that the subject of marriage came up. We knew by then it was a matter of "when" not "if."

The weekend away bolstered me for our first and only long separation. Jane had long planned a trip to Japan to visit some young women who had lived with her as foreign exchange students. Though it was extremely painful for both of us, she decided to proceed with her plans. She was away for three weeks, and I could barely stand the pain of the separation. I kept busy with work, and committed some time to Jeff, whom I had been neglecting in my devotion to Jane.

When Jane returned, our relationship continued to grow deeper and stronger. Finally the time came to tell Neva, and I asked her to meet me one last time. I drove to our parking lot rendezvous and waited anxiously in my car. Neva drove up, immediately left her car and came over to mine. She barely settled down in the passenger seat when I burst out with the news.

"I am deeply in love with Jane. The relationship between you and me is over," I blurted. I wasn't trying to be cruel, I just wanted to get the episode over as quickly as possible.

Neva said nothing. She simply opened the car door and got out. She briskly walked over to her car, unlocked the door, started her engine and drove away without a backward glance.

With a huge sense of relief, I drove to work. I finally had jumped off the seesaw I had ridden with Neva. Now I could progress with my new life without the shadow of my past.

On June 4, I made lunch reservations at El Rancho Restaurant in Evergreen, a quaint mountain town nestled in the foothills just west of Denver. It was a beautiful spring day, and the sun shone brightly in the brilliant blue sky.

We headed up Interstate 70 and soon left the city behind. The landscape changed from suburban housing developments to rolling hills dotted with pine trees and elegant mountain homes. We began climbing the steep hill that would take us into Evergreen. After we passed the Genesee exit, I pulled the car over to the shoulder of the road. I stopped at the crest of the hill, where the world-famous scenic overpass provides a picture frame for a spectacular Rocky Mountain view.

"Let's walk a little," I said.

Jane looked at me in surprise, but shook her head in agreement.

I got out of the car and went around to Jane's side to open her door. We walked a few steps along the side of the road, quietly drinking in the beauty of the mountain peaks.

I stopped, turned to Jane, and with the Rockies as our witness, I asked, "Janie, will you marry me?"

She accepted, and I lovingly placed a ring upon her finger. I drew her to me and wrapped her in my arms. We shared a passionate kiss while passing cars honked their horns, sharing in our celebration.

We continued up the mountain to El Rancho, a rustic log restaurant overlooking the pine forest, where we ate a quiet lunch, suffused in the tranquility of our happiness. The rest of the world had the soft edges of a surreal painting; we only had eyes for each other.

I wanted to make that engagement day one that Jane would never forget. Neil Diamond was in town that night, and I decided the concert would be a perfect way to cap the celebration.

The day tickets had gone on sale, I had awakened early, ready to face the crowds of Diamond fans. I told my secretary I'd be in the office around noon. I expected the lines to be long, but I was totally unprepared for the mob scene that greeted me as I arrived at the Westland Shopping Center at dawn. The line already stretched endlessly along the sidewalk around the mall's perimeter. Although I hate crowds and abhor waiting in lines, I was determined to take Jane to this concert. I took my place in line and impatiently waited for the doors to open at 10:00 a.m. The line moved laboriously around the mall and finally into the Ticketmaster outlet. I didn't reach the counter until 3:00 p.m. Finally, tickets in hand, I triumphantly went back to work.

The wait was worth it. Although we had seats in one of the highest balconies, the concert was a delight. Diamond, one of my favorite male vocalists, sang all his popular hits. My emotions were at an all-time high, and I was heady from the music and my love of Jane. It was one of the happiest days of my life.

The next two months passed swiftly as we made plans to combine our households and get married. Because the depth of our relationship shut out the rest of the world, we decided to have a very private ceremony.

I picked Jane up to marry her on Friday morning, September 2, 1983, a sunny day with a taste of fall in the air. Unlike the first time I headed to the altar, this time I had no pangs of anxiety. I knew that this was absolutely the right thing, and I was at peace. I was eager to be Jane's husband.

I was dressed in a navy blazer, and she wore a mauve silk dress. We drove down to the City and County of Denver and were wed in a judge's chambers. Jane had requested a judge she had known professionally, and a court referee she knew was our witness.

Our friends arranged for us to celebrate the marriage privately in a small dining room at Jonathan's, the site of our first date. The two of us had lunch together after the wedding, again alone in our bliss. On Saturday we left for our honeymoon in Carmel, California, where we spent a euphoric week enjoying the scenery and each other's company.

When we got back, I moved into Jane's house until we could find a home of our own. There was a house for sale on Fairfax Street, not far from where Jane lived, that she had admired from the outside a number of times. She told me about it, and we made an appointment to see it. Instantly we both fell in love with the east Denver brick home with a white picket fence around it. We made an offer on the house, and by the end of September, we were living there.

Jane brought her dog, Annie, a blonde Golden lab mix, into our new household, and I brought my old poodle, Tramp. The dogs were the only trappings of our old lives that we carried into the new marriage. We started totally anew, with new furniture for our new home.

Both of my children were in college, and they no longer came home to stay with me. Patti had decided in her freshman year that she no longer liked her name. She asked people to call her by her middle name, Michelle, and since then she has always been Michelle. She, too, had decided to start a new life.

We decided to invite all our friends to an open house over Thanksgiving weekend to celebrate our wedding and our new home. Jane and I went to great lengths, setting out a sumptuous buffet lunch. But the weather was not to cooperate. It snowed for two straight days, and blizzard conditions prevailed. The roads in Denver were impassable, and we had to cancel the party. It was a big disappointment to both of us that our friends couldn't finally share in our joy.

Jane and I continued to work on the west side of town, and we commuted together each morning. I dropped her off at Lutheran Hospital and then continued west to the office.

We could hardly bear to be apart. We dreaded the separation that Mondays brought after sharing weekends together. To ease the pain, I picked Jane up for lunch each Monday, and we drove over to the Gemini or the Wheatridge Dairy, our two favorite hangouts near the hospital. We muddled through the rest of the week by talking on the phone at least once a day.

I eagerly drove over to Lutheran to meet Jane at the end of the work day. If she had to work late or go to a meeting, I stayed at my office and finished some paperwork. I couldn't wait to be with her, to return to the haven we had created as our home.

Our time together was perfect, and I could think of nothing else I needed to make my life complete. Jane, however, had never had children, and desperately wanted them.

We began to talk seriously about the role of children in our lives after we had been married about a year. I thought my child-rearing days were over, but Jane confessed how important it was for her to be a mother. I agreed that I wanted to share the experience of having a child with her, a physical manifestation of our deep love for each other. But I also wanted to protect the uniqueness of what we had together.

We agreed that we would have a child, and we vowed that we would leave time in our relationship for just the two of us. It seemed like the best of both worlds, and we were both satisfied with the decision.

Jane became pregnant late in 1984. She was radiant in her anticipation of becoming a mother. Our son, Kevin, was born August 17, 1985, at Rose Medical Center in Denver. Jane's mother had died, but an old friend from Tulsa came up to help for the first week. Jane sank into a serious postpartum depression when her friend left. She felt alone and confused.

I arrived home from work each evening and immediately strove to relieve Jane of child care. I took over the evening feeding, and I was the one who got up during the night. I wanted Jane to have time to recover from her Caesarean-section operation and the depression that plagued her. Gradually, she regained her strength and her spirit, and we became a family of three.

I had never been more content. My career had taken a turn for the better, and I was able to provide well for my new family without working day and night. I was not only successful as a financial planner, but I also felt that I was contributing to my clients' well-being.

Insurance sales had been distasteful because I was dealing with the somber subject of death. Now, as a financial planner, I could help people get more out of life. I cared deeply about my clients' welfare, and it showed. My business continued to grow as clients referred their friends. Work was gratifying for the first time since I left the Home, and I was rewarded financially as well. My older children, Jeff and Michelle, were also on their way to successful careers — Jeff as an attorney and Michelle as a broadcaster.

I was nurtured by the happiness of my work and home lives, and my sentimental side came into full bloom. I showered Jane with cards and gifts, but my coup de grace came with her fortieth birthday in December 1989. She had hinted that she wanted to celebrate with a party, so a few months before her birthday, I asked her best friends, Pam, Dixie, Tom and Colleen, and her sister, Susan, to lunch at Writer's Manor, a well-known south Denver restaurant located in a hotel lobby. We sat at a large, round, wooden table and brainstormed ideas while we enjoyed the excellent food. We decided to go back and do some research, then reconnect for lunch in two weeks.

Dixie came to the next lunch with an idea that I immediately and totally embraced. She had heard about a glass-topped train car that could be attached to an Amtrak locomotive and taken into the mountains. The mountains, where I had proposed to Jane, held much symbolism for me. I could think of no better way to celebrate her birthday. I booked the train to take sixteen of us to Glenwood Springs, the mountain resort town renowned for its hot springs pools, and made reservations for us to stay at the Hotel Denver, located across the street from the train station.

The lunch group continued to meet every other Monday to hammer out the details. We planned every intricacy of the weekend, including what Jane would wear for her dinner party Saturday night. The scenario called for me to take Jane to a hotel on Friday night. After we left, Pam would come to the house and gather up the clothes Jane would need for the trip, including her party outfit.

I surreptitiously went through Jane's things to make sure everything in order. To my despair, I couldn't find the black pantyhose she always wore with the dress we had planned for Saturday night.

"Where are your black pantyhose?" I asked her.

She looked at me quizzically, and said, "I think they're in the laundry."

The next day, I looked again. They were still missing.

"Where are your black pantyhose?" I asked again.

Jane shot a look of confusion mixed with anger my way.

"Why in the hell do you want to know where my black pantyhose are? You're driving me crazy," she said incredulously.

I decided that I'd better back off, or I might expose my secret plans. Instead of pursuing the matter further, I called Pam and asked her to buy Jane a new pair of black hose.

I told Jane we were going to have a night away from home, and I ordered a limousine for the occasion. The limousine took us to the Oxford Hotel in Denver, originally opened in 1891 as a luxury hotel for those who made their fortune in the Colorado mines. The historic hotel had fallen into hard times in the 1960s and 1970s, but in 1983 a $12-million project had restored its original elegance while adding modern amenities. The Oxford was once again one of Denver's crown jewels. We had a lovely dinner in the hotel dining room, then retired to our antique-laden room.

The next morning, I awoke full of anxiety. I was having great difficulty keeping the party a secret, and I was scared something would happen to spoil it. I couldn't wait to get going.

"Are you ready yet, Janie? When are you going to be ready?" I asked over and over as she put on her makeup.

Jane looked at me with exasperation, wondering why I was in such a rush.

"I know I'm driving you crazy. I'm going to take a little walk and come back so you can get ready in peace," I finally said. Jane agreed that was a great idea.

Unbeknownst to her, I was going to make sure everything was in order. My compulsive need for perfection led me to Union Station, just a block from the hotel, where I could assure myself that all was going according to plan.

When I returned to the Oxford, Jane

Eric and Jane get ready for a night on the town.

was finally ready, and we went outside and got into the limousine. I had been in a rush, but now we had some extra time on our hands. I wanted to stall so all the guests could arrive before we did. I had the driver cruise slowly around the streets of Denver rather than drive directly the short block to the train station. Jane was totally perplexed about what we were doing; she thought we were going to pick out the new car she so desperately needed. Finally I told the driver to go to Union Station.

"I have a new friend that I made in the last six months, and he has this train car that he's refurbished. I'd really like for you to see it," I blurted to Jane. I had carefully rehearsed the line for weeks.

Jane looked at me askance. Considering how I shared everything in my life with her, she wondered how it was possible that I had a new friend that I had never mentioned. She was beginning to get very suspicious, but she decided to play along.

"All right, Eric, I'd love to meet your new friend," Jane said.

I took her by the hand, and with quiet determination, led her into the ornate, high-ceilinged train station. Our footsteps echoed on the tile floor of the expansive waiting room, filled with wooden benches. The station was practically deserted, and we crossed the length of the huge room and headed down the stairs to the tracks in silence. I was engrossed in pulling off the surprise, and Jane was totally befuddled by the turn of events.

Ours was the only train on the tracks, and we walked to the far end where the glass-topped car was attached. I climbed the stairs of the train with Jane following close behind.

"Bill, Bill, are you here?" I shouted.

Then we rounded the corner, and Jane got a glimpse of all her friends. Her best friend, Pam, was there, and Dixie and Tom and Colleen and Susan and J.W. Her cousin, Patty, from Dallas was on board, and so was Jane, her best childhood friend from Tulsa. My daughter, Michelle, was also on hand.

The car was decorated with black and white balloons, and there was a computer printout that said, "Over the Hill."

Jane was still in shock when someone shouted, "Do you get it yet, Janie?"

"No, I don't get it," she answered.

"We're all taking this train to Glenwood Springs for a weekend party to celebrate your birthday," a friend shouted.

Jane flushed with surprise. She was overwhelmed by the magnitude of the effort we had put into planning the surprise.

The weekend was a stupendous success. Tom had put together tapes for us to listen to on the train, everything from Rachmaninoff to the Beach Boys. He also found a country western song, "Take Me Back to Tulsa, I'm Too Young to Marry." Because Tulsa is Jane's hometown, it became the theme song of the weekend. The spectacular Rockies rolled by the train windows while we danced, sang and laughed for the four-and-a-half hour ride to Glenwood. The glass-topped train gave us an unobstructed view of dramatic Glenwood Canyon, with its 1,800-foot granite walls sculpted by the Colorado River.

We strolled arm-in-arm from the train station across the street to Hotel Denver, intoxicated from the gaiety of our train ride. A tastefully decorated Christmas tree towered over the check-in desk in the hotel lobby, adding to the spirit of festivity that suffused us. The hotel, built in 1906, had been modernized, and the rooms were cozy and comfortable.

I rented the banquet room at the hotel, and that night we had a private birthday party for Jane. The sixteen of us sat around a large square table covered with fine linen table clothes garnished with Christmas greens and red ribbons. Tom and Colleen took us on a sentimental journey with their slide show, "This Is Your Life, Jane Cahn."

Surrounded by the love of her friends and family, Jane was on top of the world. I, watching her happiness, basked in the glow she emitted. I had wanted to give her an experience that would turn into a lifetime memory, and I had succeeded.

When we returned, the planning committee had one last lunch together, and we invited Jane. The committee presented us with a beautiful silver and brass photo album documenting the weekend. The album was engraved, "For Eric, From the Committee."

Another emotional high occurred later that month. Jane and I had gone out Christmas shopping and returned to find a message on our telephone recorder from a Peter Koch in California.

"I am looking for an Eric Cahn who came to America in 1950. If you are that person, please call me back because I'm your cousin," the voice on the recorder said.

I called immediately, and I learned that he was the son of Vater's older sister, Rosa. He told me that Rosa had married a Christian, Nikolaus Koch, and had three children. Peter was the eldest of the three. We made plans to have him visit us when he came to Denver the following February.

Peter arrived in Denver, and I met him at the airport with eagerness. I could hardly wait to see this cousin, my first contact with the Cahn family for over a decade.

Peter reminded me that Vater was the fifth of eight children, only one of whom, Trude, was still living. Two of the eight had perished in the Holocaust — Leo died in Bergen Belsen along with his wife and ten-year-old son, and Hilde died in Auschwitz. The stories gave me goose bumps. I wondered if Vater and Hilde had been in Auschwitz at the same time. Had he seen his sister perish as he had witnessed his wife's death?

The rest of the Cahns were scattered by the winds of war. While Rosa, Trude and Julius, my Vater, remained in Germany, the others wound up in Israel, Morocco and England.

Peter spent several hours at our home, telling us stories that swept me into a tidal wave of emotions. Memories of Vater and my aunts from the days in Leutesdorf came flooding back for the first time in decades. I had felt like an orphan for so long; now Peter was providing me with family.

I wanted to hold on to this thin thread connecting me to my childhood, and I wrote to Peter soon after he returned to California. All the letters I sent mysteriously came back, marked "addressee unknown." Peter has sent Kevin a card or gift occasionally over the years, but he never provides a return address. And he has never called me again.

Once more a member of the Cahn family abandoned me, evoking bitter memories of waiting for letters from Vater as a twelve-year-old boy in Pueblo. Once again I lost the chance to recover memories from my past that affected my life as an adult. But Peter had piqued my interest, and I was determined not to give up this time. I would search for other avenues to self-discovery.

Chapter Sixteen

A Lifetime of Tomorrows

After Neva and I separated, I had started counseling to help me through the difficult process of rebirth. I finally began to unpeel the protective layers that shielded me from my past with the help of group therapy. I shared my childhood with the group, and they encouraged me to learn more.

So in the early 1980s I began writing to the French and German consulates and the Oeuvre de Secours to see what I could learn about my past. It was then that I received copies of the correspondence that Opa and Vater had written to the French in their successful attempt to find me after the war.

I also tried, without success, to find the French Christian family that had hidden me. The French government was helpful, but every lead turned into a dead end. I have been unable to fulfill my dream of thanking the family who saved my life.

Jane encouraged me to continue my quest to learn more about my past. We spent hours talking about my feelings, and I began to get a glimpse of how my early experiences had affected my life.

I became more comfortable with my history, and I was able to discuss it with others. I met Michael Allen at the Center for Judaic Studies at the University of Denver, and he asked me to speak to school children about my life under the Nazis. I agreed, and I began making a few speeches around the Denver area.

I developed a presentation that helped students transport themselves to the world of Jews in Germany in the 1930s. I asked the students to close their eyes and imagine losing their rights. First, they had to remember to put on a yellow armband before they could leave the house in the morning. Then they could no longer shop in the local grocery store. Finally they were told they couldn't come to school any more.

After setting the stage, I told them my story: How my family and I were carted off to Camp Gurs in a smelly, crowded rail car. How we lived in squalid conditions with little food and water. How I was taken from my parents at the age of four and hidden in a stranger's basement for safekeeping. How my parents were taken off to Auschwitz, and my mother was sent directly to the gas chambers to die.

The students listened in silence. They stared at me in disbelief as I told the story. When I finished, I asked for questions, and the small hands darted upward. The spellbound students rattled off questions as they tried to fathom the horrors of my childhood.

"What happened to your father?"

"What did you do in the basement?"

"What did you eat?"

"Do you remember anything about your mother?"

I quietly answered each question, impressed with the depth of their empathy. I left each speech feeling like a pricked balloon.

All my strength had been drained from me with the effort of the talk. But it was also a catharsis. With each retelling of my story, I gained a deeper understanding of its effects on my adult life.

And I felt the work was important. Children viewed television reports of genocide daily from around the world, and it seemed somehow far away and unreal. It was crucial for them to discover the true horror by hearing how it affected a real person. I was doing at least a small part to make the atrocities of history come alive. Maybe it would make a difference in how young people saw and treated the world.

While I was revealing myself through these speeches, I was still on a solo journey. I had never talked to another child survivor, and I didn't know if my feelings and experience were unique or common.

Then in August 1990 my old friend Judy Lazar found an article about the first ever Hidden Child Conference planned for New York in 1991. I was immediately fascinated and wrote for information.

The marketing letter from the conference organizers read, "The goals of this Gathering are to enable us to recall the past, to understand how our experiences have shaped our present and future lives and to help one another recall and share events some of us were too young to remember."

It sounded exactly like what I needed at this time in my life. Jane said she would be glad to come along if I decided to attend. I was determined to face the ghosts of my past, so I made conference reservations and bought airline tickets well in advance. I began to tremble with a spiraling chill of panic as the conference drew near.

"You know, Janie, I don't think I want to do this. This event is really not for me," I told her one evening in March, two months before the conference was to begin.

"Let's not make any rash decisions or cancel any reservations," Jane counseled. "See how you feel about it in the next few weeks."

Jane and I continued to discuss the trip. My mind churned with a torrent of questions: Do I really want to meet all these other people who were hidden in the war? What safely buried memories will come to the surface? Will I be able to handle them? Why am I exposing myself to so much potential pain? Isn't it best to let bygones be bygones and keep the past behind me?

On the other hand, I was filled with curiosity. How had other hidden children learned to live in the world? Were their fears of abandonment similar to mine? How did they handle family life? Have they found the families that hid them?

Finally, I decided I had to go on this self-exploratory journey. I hoped that through the pain, I would develop perspective about my life.

My daughter, Michelle, sent me a diary for my birthday so I could record my feelings during the conference. She wrote on the first page, supporting my decision to attend the conference. "It is a tremendous step for you, and I am very proud..."

I began my first entry in the diary on May 24, 1991, as we were flying above the Mississippi River. The memory of another plane ride rose from the depths of my mind, the flight forty-one years earlier when I left Germany to come to America. I entered the remembrance in my diary, recalling "the tremendous sadness and unhappiness at having my life turned upside down again and crying just before arriving in New York."

Now I was heading in the opposite direction, back to New York, to reacquaint myself with the child who had come to America those many years ago.

Jane and I did some sightseeing in New York before the conference started. We took the subway, then the ferry to Ellis

Island to revisit my first stop in America. As we toured the island, it evoked scenes of my arrival in New York and my first visit with Esther and Simon. I could almost taste the sweetness of the candy they had brought and the bitterness of how my indulgence became a family legend. I was afraid I might drown in the torrent of memories that swiftly flooded over me.

Then the conference, the First International Gathering of Children Hidden During World War II, began. A bulletin board filled with messages helped the 1,600 attenders make contact with others who had been in the same places during the war. I tacked my note on the board, "Anyone who had been in Camp Gurs, 1940-42, or in Busancais, France, please call my room, 1460."

That night, when we returned to the hotel from a Broadway show, there was a message from a woman named Eve Boden. She was in Camp Gurs and had come from Mannheim! The next day, May 26, we met to recount our stories. She told us that she was among the last to get out of France and to America in 1942. I had never before shared my story with someone who had actually been in the same squalid places at the same time. I felt like I had met a long-lost friend.

Meeting Eve was only a part of the emotional intensity that rocked my soul that day. I cried as hidden children in the morning session talked about their experiences, and I wept during lunch where Yaffa Eliach, a professor at Brooklyn College, shared her story.

I attended a workshop in the afternoon called "Fear of Abandonment." It was eye-opening to see the commonalities in the lives of the hidden children. So many of our feelings seemed to sprout from those early years away from our parents, and we were all learning to cope now in middle age.

I made several other connections with people born in Mannheim who had been sent to Gurs. The conference wrapped

Eric with children Jeff, Michelle and Kevin in December 1990.

me in a cocoon of soul mates. For all these years I thought I was journeying alone when in reality there were thousands like me.

I was overwhelmed by the power of the camaraderie when the most amazing thing happened. I came into a meeting room for those who had been in France during the war, and a woman came rushing over to me.

"I know you," she shouted. "You were in the orphanage with me after the war!"

She introduced herself as Hermine Markovitz and said she recognized me by my intense blue eyes. "Your eyes are the same as they were then," she said. She told me she had a number of photographs with her, and she thought I might be in one of them. We made plans to get together later that day.

It was a miracle. Hermine had been eighteen at the time I was in the orphanage at Draveil, and she took care of some of the younger kids like me. As we began going through her photographs, we found one of me. I had a copy of the very same photo! The French had sent it to me when I wrote for information in the early 1980s. I looked at the child I had left behind and quivered.

Each meeting created a hunger to learn more. I fed on the feast of workshops that drew me into the past. I attended a lecture by Serge Klarsfeld, who had written the book about the convoys to Auschwitz where I found my parents listed. I went to sessions on "Understanding the Hiding Experience" and "Learning to Trust and Feeling Safe." And I videotaped my story for the Jewish Heritage Museum in New York.

When the conference drew to a close, I had difficulty leaving. I wrote in my diary, "I am leaving myself behind — the hidden child who allowed himself to be who he really is for two days with 1,500 others like him."

Jane was finishing packing to go home, and I decided to take a walk around the hotel to release some of my emotional energy. I stopped back on the fifth, sixth and seventh floors of the Marriott Marquis where the conference had been. It was all gone. There were no traces of the people who had shared the two days with me, the bulletin board stuffed with messages, the flyers and books. All had disappeared into memory. I sobbed as I surveyed the still, cold convention hall.

I wept again when I returned to our room to help Jane finish packing. She talked about going home together and continuing to grow from what we had learned. I felt the sorrow of having hidden myself from friends and family for so many years. I had truly come out of hiding for the first time this weekend.

Now it was time to reveal myself to others. As soon as I returned home, I called Jeff and Michelle to share my experiences with them. Then I had lunch and talked with the people at my office. I was encouraged by the high level of support and understanding they showed.

I was eager to preserve the fragile connections I had made with my past, and I immediately wrote letters and sent pictures to Hermine Markovitz and others who had been in Mannheim and Gurs.

Memories flooded back at odd times during my work day, and I found my eyes welling up with tears. At night, my unconscious was hard at work processing what I had learned. I began having nightmares, but I could not remember them when I awoke full of angst.

The emotions continued to crash over me like tidal waves as I opened up to myself and others. Every day I felt the reality of being a hidden child and survivor. Now that I had started down this road to self-discovery, I yearned to continue my travels. But I needed a compass to guide my way.

The organizers of the conference were very wise; they realized they were helping people open a tightly locked door and that we would need continued support. One of the things they suggested was that participants start a local support group when they got home.

I immediately embraced the idea of a support group. Jane and I went through the roster of conference attenders to see if any were from Denver. We found one other person, a woman named Francie.

A week after returning home, I began thumbing through the Denver phone book, calling all those with Francie's last name. One night, I reached a message machine. The woman on the other end had a European accent, and I hoped it was Francie. It was!

She returned my call, and she told me that she did not stay at the conference because it wasn't worthwhile for her. She told me she was born in Paris and had fled to Switzerland with her mother during the war. They were hidden by a farming family, and she and her older sister came to America in 1947. We agreed to meet for lunch and talk about starting a support group.

Meanwhile, I continued revealing myself as a Holocaust survivor. When a teacher in a suburban school district was accused of calling the Nazi atrocity a "Holohoax," I was horrified. I penned a letter to the editor of the *Denver Post*, and it was published, bringing responses from friends and acquaintances. One woman stopped me in the hall at Lutheran Hospital, where I had gone on business, to tell me her father had helped liberate Dachau.

Jane and I met Francie and her husband for lunch, and we talked about starting a Hidden Child Group. Nothing happened, however, until I received another fortuitous phone call.

Ilana Zandell called me one Sunday morning and said she had been a hidden child in Lithuania. Although she hadn't attended the conference in New York, a cousin of hers had. The cousin had given Ilana my name, and she was eager to meet me.

On Monday, July 1, 1991, Jane and I met Ilana for lunch. There was an instant connection, and we were able to open our hearts to each other. She shared that she was hidden in an orphanage in Lithuania, and her father survived Dachau. Her mother was in a ghetto in Lithuania and died of starvation a month before liberation. After the war, Ilana was found by an aunt, who then reunited her with her father in Munich. She and her father came to America together.

I marveled at the parallels in our stories. We had both lost our mothers, and our fathers had survived. Both of us had been liberated and sent to orphanages, to be found by relatives. But while Ilana was lucky enough to come to America with her father, I had left my Vater behind in Germany.

Ilana and I talked seriously about looking for other child survivors so we could start a support group. I lent her the audiotapes of the Hidden Child Conference so she could share some of what I had experienced.

Ilana phoned me immediately after listening to the tapes. The power of the conference inspired her, and we decided to go forward with our plan to start a support group. A friend of Ilana's, Otto Verdoner, joined our planning committee.

We developed a flyer announcing our first meeting at 7:00 p.m. September 26, 1991, at Temple Emanuel. The three of us visited the Denver synagogues to distribute the announcement.

I was sick with worry when the night of the meeting came. I had put my soul on the line, and I didn't know what to expect. How heartwarming it was when eleven survivors came to the temple to tell their stories. We used the model of the Hidden Child Conference, and we asked the participants — eleven strangers — to share their experiences during the war.

We were moved by the level of openness that these survivors showed. Immediately, people began to talk about themselves because they felt protected by the blanket of our shared circumstances. The meeting was a success, and word of our group spread.

Our group now has grown to twenty-six, and we continue to meet monthly. Carole Kornreich, a psychiatrist, volunteers to facilitate our discussions.

I had lunch with Cindy Silverman of the Anti-Defamation League to advertise our group to a wider audience. Cindy mentioned that ADL has a speaker's bureau and invited me to join. I immediately agreed. This time, my shyness didn't get in the way because of the potent impact the conference had made on my life. I felt a desire and an obligation to share my story.

Now I began my career as a public speaker in earnest. Cindy called me often, and I rarely refused. I talked to men's clubs and church groups, but most of all I talked to school children. More than 10,000 young people and adults heard my story in the three years following the conference.

The telling of my tale is powerful not only for my audience, but also for me. I can talk of my mother's death in Auschwitz without shedding a visible tear, but I am sobbing on the inside. Often when I leave a speaking engagement, I cry in the car on the way back to my office.

Once back in my office, I visit my mother's corner. It is a place where I can regain my strength and feel the power of her love in my life.

I make a vow while I stand there thinking about her short and painful story. I promise my mother that I will continue to bear witness to her experience so that her death will not be in vain. Maybe if enough children hear her story, they will help make our world a place where genocide ceases. Maybe by telling about her life, I will help save other mothers.

Finally, I give thanks. I acknowledge the difficult decision my mother made over fifty years ago, relinquishing her children to an unknown fate. It was her faith in a better tomorrow that brought me to where I am today. Through her ultimate sacrifice, she granted me a lifetime of tomorrows.